The Great Australian Shed

An Improvised Life

'the true blues'

Copyright ©2016

Writing as 'the true blues,' are the following authors: © Linda Ruth Brooks; © Graeme Brown; © Peter Bullock; ©Graeme Frauenfelder © Martin Killips; © Tony Lang; ©Marilyn Linn; ©John McBride; © Al Mewett; © Ron McKinnon; © Murray McLeod; ©Victoria Norton; © Barrie Ridgway; © Lowell Tarling; © ; © George Townsend; ©James Ward; © Matthew Glenn Ward; © Peter Wilson

All rights reserved. This book is copyright protected. Apart from any fair dealings for the purpose of private study, criticism, research or review as permitted under the *Copyright Act (Australia)*, no part may be reproduced by any process without written permission. Enquiries should be addressed to the publisher.

Australiana/Australian history/memoir

ISBN- 978-0-6481902-2-6
A copy of this book can be found in the National Library of Australia.

By their inclusion here, each author and artist claims and maintains individual copyright of their work/s. This includes the right to publish their individual works in any other publication. Individual contributors are legally liable for their own content; no personal responsibility is accepted by the publisher. Every attempt has been made by authors to give appropriate acknowledgments for their material, visual or written.

To Australian life

Contents

Introduction 1
George Townsend 4
    The Cultivation 5
    Our Humble Abode 8
    The Great Australian Shed 13
    Fishin' 19
    Dreams Lonely in the Night 21
    Tribal Law 23
    Has-beens of the Rodeo 24
    Rusty iron... worn out dingo traps 25
    Toyota Dreaming 27
Tony Lang 28
    Young Love, First Love 29
    Privations of an Army Padre 32
    The Magic Mist 35
    The story behind the Magic Mist 37
    The Day an APC* Flew 38
    The Spider Queen 43
    Dream Sheep 40
    My Prostate Op 41
Al Mewett 44
    Sitting in Bligh's Chair 45
    Grace Bros Australia 51
    For Valour 57
Lowell Tarling 62
    To Catch a Thief 63
    Jam Studio, Gosford 75
Murray McLeod 80
    Lt. Frank McNamara VC, Flying ace 81
    Ken Rosewall 83
    Ken Kavanagh, Aussie racing legend 86
    W/Cdr. Hughie Edwards 91
    Pacific Conquest 1928 95
Matthew Glenn Ward 100
    The Great Homework Swindle 101
    Missing the Newcastle Earthquake 104
    A Labrador goes shopping! - 109
Graeme Frauenfelder 114
    Send in the Clown 115

John McBride 118
    Kitchen table, heart of the Aussie home 119
    I remember the Kokoda Track 123
    Two tone shoes 128

James Ward 132
    The Blackfella Wisdom of Albert 133
    Desert 136
    Longing For Beaches 136
    The Old Homestead 138
    I Loved a Young Girl Once 139
    Our Parting 140
    The Channon* 141

Barrie Ridgway 142
    My first customer 143
    The "black" kangaroo 145
    Mrs Pierson's frequent visits 147
    Wartime fishing trip 149

Graeme Brown 152
    Dad's Orchard 153

Martin Killips 156
    Lost For Words! 157
    To Counting Spells 159
    Nice Is Really Nice! – Martin Killips 160
    Hypochondriac! 163
    Just A Minute! 165

Ron McKinnon 166
    Opening time at the Garage 167

Peter Bullock 168
    Woodcutting and "gelly" 169
    Cracker night on Mulberry Farm 171

Marilyn Linn 174
    Valley of the Winds 175
    The Call of the Wild 179
    Asparagus 182

Victoria Norton 184
    The Cockie's Mother & the Hired Hand 185

Linda Ruth Brooks 190
    "Steptoe and Son" 191
    Dad's apprentice 196
    "Underbelly" comes to the suburbs 203

Fireball	208
The Great Escape	212
Northern Territory	216
Australia	217
Billabong	219
Peter Wilson	220
Nev – A True Mate	221
The Settler's Tale	222
The Black of Night	223

Introduction

Along the journey of my unconventional childhood, I was introduced to the "great Australian shed". As Australians, we are excessively fond of our sheds. My theory regarding this lies in our convict heritage. After all, we arrived in this harsh land, with nothing but the chains on our feet. The ships that brought us here carried more guns and soldiers than tools. Ingenuity was mandatory. If the aristocracy had arrived without the convict element they would soon have died; manual labour was of more value in this new land than following the correct morning-tea rituals or organising a fox hunt. Of course, it's only a theory.

At first, when very young, I thought the shed was where Dad hid from Mum. Later on, I discovered that although there may have been some truth to this assumption, there was so much more to Dad's shed.

It was chock full of useful tools Dad used to make marvellous things. I was constantly fascinated and often joined him there. The fact it was a place of gentle harmony added to the appeal.

Mum would get up a full head of steam to tackle the housework, taking on the mantle of martyred slavery. Mops, buckets and vacuum cleaners would appear. Dad would stand near the back door and clear his throat.

'I'm just ducking out to the shed, Else,' he'd say.

I would stand next to him.

'I'm duckin' too,' I'd add, holding my breath and crossing my fingers. Escape was so near but so far. Because we were both deemed hopeless at assisting Mum in the housework that began at dawn and ended at midnight, she'd let us go with a weary sigh.

Mum seemed afraid of the shed, with its smells of metal, the noise and sparks of the welding machine and the oil and grime. I remember her storming in there only once, and promptly putting her foot in the sump oil Dad was recycling. She gave us a short speech on the filth of the pair of us, and the dangers of dirt in general, but as she was discomforted by an oily foot she very soon left us to our mess.

I wondered on this occasion, as I had on many others, if these incidents were not quite as accidental as they appeared, but strategies of my father to discourage her from entering his domain. He wouldn't have been the only male in history to do so. He gave no sign of this, but at times he could be inscrutable.

Dad was orderly and precise. He enjoyed his world of tools and tinkering immensely, whistling as he worked.

On the shed wall was a Masonite board with hooks and holes and the outline of whatever belonged there. In my mind the shed was a tidy place although every bench was cluttered with projects in various stages of completion, unlike inside where not a crumb was allowed to linger on floor or table.

The shed was a different kind of *tidy* than inside the house. His tools were always in their proper place in his own system. Engine parts, gas bottles and cables were allowed on the floor, but he never misplaced anything.

Dad made wrought iron gates and trims. All our car repairs were undertaken by him, and later by my brother. There were tyres he was re-treading, deepening the groove with a hot electric thing that looked like a soldering iron. I can't even remember what it was called because I learned very little about the things he did, and much about the patient focus with which he approached each task.

Dad kept his tools clean with a kerosene soaked rag. He had an old peach tin with an inch of kerosene and a rag. This was a job I often requested, just to be near him. I sat quietly on the floor making sure all the grime was wiped off his tools or engine parts.

If Mum had bothered to look, she would have been shocked to see me curled up contentedly on the rough cement floor, quietly and diligently polishing Dad's tools.

Just under the ceiling of the shed Dad had positioned wire meshing the length and breadth of the shed. He hung lights from this in various positions to illuminate whatever part of the car engine he was currently fixing. Although this marvellous system served his lighting purposes effectively, he allowed me to think I was indispensable by holding the torch for him. I would do this for hours, shining the beam exactly where he needed it, while he talked about gearboxes and how to care for them so the gears wouldn't grind and shear off. He explained pistons, talked about carburettors and how the clutch worked.

Never quite grasping his skills or passion for those things—I did learn about life and unconditional love within these lessons about machinery and tools. I learned that if you wanted something to last you had to take care of it.

Among the vices, electric saws, spanners, nuts and bolts, there were always collections of paint cans and airbrushes. Dad made signs for the church notice board and pungent paint fumes filled the shed, along with the smells of the welder. There were several soldering irons and grinders that filled the air with the smell of metal shavings and hot molten solder.

It was a wonder we weren't a bit high on the cacophony of smells. We were certainly happy out there. Many years later, after his death, I visited Sovereign Hill, in Victoria and stood transfixed with unexpected tears when I walked into Ye Olde Blacksmith's.

It smelled like home.

Linda Ruth Brooks

George Townsend

George Townsend is a prolific poet and writes descriptive, lively short stories. His first published work was a family history *Our Crew*. Watch out for his debut novel *Deranged*, about his time as a park ranger.

The Cultivation

We were clearing a paddock. Or at least Dad was. Along with the neighbours we were using gelignite. Gelignite was easy to obtain in those days along with detonators and fuses. The local hardware store sold the lot. So loud explosions and the crashing sound of trees falling were often heard in our neighbourhood. Sometimes clods of earth or bits of wood clattered on our roof.

The hardware store also sold saddles and everything else that was useful on a farm including fencing wire, both barbed and plain, staples, pliers, in fact everything you'd ever want including groceries. We kids could even buy broken biscuits. For a penny obtained from Mum we could purchase a big bag of broken biscuits which we ate sitting in the back of the truck going home.

With the gelignite, Dad was blowing out trees and stumps from the paddocks needed for cultivation. It was later discovered that one of the crops planted was only beneficial to the local wallabies. We had the fattest wallabies in the district.

Holes were dug beneath the offending tree or stump. Gelignite came in greasy sticks and a stick was placed into each hole and then a detonator was pushed into the stick. A length of black fuse was attached to the hollow end of the detonator. Black powder fuse was yellow in colour and burnt at around one foot per minute. So you could calculate how long you had to seek cover after the fuse was lit. The hole was back-filled with clay and earth and the fuse lit. And every one took cover!

A big bloodwood tree stood out in the middle of the paddock. In Dad's mind it had to go. So "we" dug a hole down underneath it. Or at least Dad did. We kids were pretty keen to help until hard work was involved. Shovels were like black snakes in our minds, not to be touched. But we were all keen to get our hands on gelignite, detonators, fuse and matches. *That* we knew a lot about. Or so we thought.

The hole was dug, explosive in place, the fuse lit, and we all took cover. The fuse spat and sputtered. It emitted smoke, then the smoke vanished down into the hole. We waited, nothing. And we waited a bit more. Still nothing. Maybe the fuse had "gone out" before reaching the detonator. But we couldn't be sure. We waited some more. Still nothing. We slunk inside and waited. Still nothing.

Next day we tiptoed around and kept away from the tree. We walked "quietly" in case heavy footfalls set the gelignite off. And we waited, expecting a loud explosion, clouds of dust, dirt and a falling tree at any moment. None of which happened. It was time for a new tack.

That afternoon Dad carefully dug a hole down beside the explosives and set another charge. He did this carefully. I can feel now, sixty odd years later, the trepidation he must have felt. He set the charge and lit the fuse. We took cover. With a loud bang the gelignite exploded. The tree launched itself up a few feet and slowly toppled over. And we all cheered. Even the wallabies rejoiced, knowing the bounty to come.

After all the trees and stumps had been blown out of the ground we had to set about removing them. Suitable trees were cut into fence post lengths with a cross-cut saw and split into posts using a fourteen pound hammer and steel wedges. I was usually on one end of the saw with Dad at the opposite end. Logs were rolled in together. Sticks were gathered and fires set. Roots that were left behind were grubbed and cut below cultivation level. After the ground was cleared and the unwanted timber was burned or rolled out of the way the paddock was ready for cultivation.

Old Flarey lived down the road, he was a market gardener with a lot of "knowledge" and a rotary hoe. He was also a Professor of Phrenology and had handbills to prove it. For a small fee he could "read your head" and tell by the bumps he felt with gnarled old fingers what your destiny was. He could tell whether you would be a farmer, a doctor, a tradesman or a layabout. I reckon the bumps on a politician's head would be the same as those on a scoundrel's. Be hard to tell the difference.

Old Flarey was of an indeterminate age but he had to be at least seventy. Around he would come with his old Howard rotary hoe which he would put to work cultivating our paddock. What a sight it was with its two steel wheels bucking and kicking across the paddock with Flarey gamely holding on to it!

When it hit a piece of buried timber it pig-rooted like a fresh horse. Our job was to walk behind and pick up the sticks it unearthed and stack them in piles for burning. We weren't allowed to use the rotary hoe, so our interest in market gardening soon waned. We thought our parents were very selfish to deny us the fun side of market gardening, never allowing us to use gelignite or have a go on the rotary hoe. So every chance we got we'd sneak off, only to be hauled back to work.

Our Humble Abode

We lived in a shack out the back of Warnervale when Warnervale was trees and scrub not covered with the mansions that are there today. Dad had plans that one day the shack would evolve, through his hard work, into a house. At night time candles and kerosene lamps lit up our home. Electricity had yet to arrive in Warnervale. Water came from a tank, and when the tank was dry was carried up from the creek in buckets. There were no telephones and few close neighbours so we pretty well kept to ourselves. Our schooling was by correspondence until 1958 when a one teacher school was established a couple of miles away.

Dad was a builder. He was always building something, a shed, cow bail, fence or our house. His building was done mostly on weekends. During the week he was a fettler on the railways. Fettler's looked after the "permanent way", the rail tracks. When he wasn't building he was pulling down what he had erected the week before. Dad's main building project was building us a house.

The house he has planned for us was L-shaped probably because Mum's first name is Linda. It must have been difficult to build because he put a lot of time and effort into it. He also purchased a lot of timber which he stacked up on the ground and covered with black plastic. Termites displayed a lot of interest in Dad's building, especially the timber he bought home.

Some weekends he would devote his energy to pulling down a wall. There was never enough time in a weekend to both pull down a wall and erect a new one in its place. At the end of the day he would nail black plastic or a tarp up to keep out the weather. Our weather was very resourceful and still found its way in.

Mum was a keen gardener and would sometimes plant a shrub up against the house where Dad had pulled down a wall. The shrub would grow and eventually enter the house through the space where a wall should be. Dad would have to prune the shrub to erect the new wall. Mum objected to Dad's pruning and would call him a 'bloody bastard'. Dad would then leave that section of the house and start somewhere else. Our house was a "works in progress".

I hated having to help Dad and would try and make myself scarce on weekends when Dad was building. Sometimes I got caught and would have to help. Dad would be up the ladder and say 'pass me that piece of timber' and point in the general direction of a stack of timber. I would grab one and he would say 'Not that one, the one over there' and wave his arms around 360 degrees of the compass.

Invariably the second piece I grabbed was wrong. He would say harsh words and I bolted. He would request a handful of 3 inch nails; I would pass up the wrong size and get yelled at all over again. On one occasion Dad was up the ladder nailing and swearing. I had an old axe which I was hacking into the top of a stump. Dad's carpenter's rule was sitting on the stump. Suddenly the rule "moved" under the descending axe head and found itself in two pieces. I pushed the two pieces together and "made myself scarce" for the rest of the weekend.

Our house only had a part floor. The bearers and joists were in place, Dad only had enough flooring for a part. This was ideal for us, we could drop unwanted food, such as turnips down through the holes without Mum being aware we hadn't eaten them. For a door we had a sheet of canvas nailed across the doorway. On windy days bricks were used to hold it down and keep the cold and rain out. We had running water—When it rained water ran in through holes in the roof and was collected in tins and buckets placed under the drips. Some day we would have a roof that didn't leak and a door.

My brother and I shared a bedroom. This was an "add on", an extension attached to the main building. We had a floor and walls but no door. The guttering from the "main house" ran through our bedroom into the water tank. During heavy rain it overflowed. Not many kids had a water feature in their bedroom.

Mum cooked on an old fuel stove. Our job was to keep up a supply of firewood. One day the bottom of the stove burned out and the resultant spill of hot coals threatened to destroy our humble abode. The stove was moved outside under a tree and Mum cooked on that. When it rained she laid a sheet of corrugated iron across the top of the stove balanced on whatever saucepans or pots she happened to be cooking in. This kept the rain from putting out the fire. Mum is a resourceful woman. One day Dad planned to build a kitchen and install a new stove.

Our combined laundry shower room was outside and it too didn't have a door. In winter a quick dash along a muddy path to the shower and back was the order of the day. We had an outside dunny, a pan inside a corrugated iron structure. A favourite trick of mine was to wait until someone settled inside and then "stone" the dunny. But I had to be careful. If I stoned the dunny when a parent was inside all hell would break loose. A preferred target was my brother or one of my sisters. However I frequently got into trouble for this trick.

When the pan was full it was our job to dig a hole down the back and bury the contents. Not a pleasant task.

Mum always put a lot of effort into Christmas. A few months before she would make boiled puddings to be eaten on Christmas day and onwards while ever they lasted. This involved placing dried fruit into a bowl, adding brandy and allowing the fruit to soak overnight. Dad usually added the brandy; some of it went into the bowl of fruit. Next day the other ingredients were added, flour, eggs sugar and the whole lot mixed. The resulting mix was wrapped in cloths and boiled in a pot placed over the fuel stove. Our job was to keep a plentiful supply of wood up to Mum. I learned early in life that if you give a woman one piece of wood they will make that last all day, give them a wood bin full they will burn that in a day. After cooking the puddings were hang from the rafters (our home did not have ceilings) usually where you could bump your head on them as you walked past.

Christmas shopping was always high on Mum's agenda. She would pack us all onto the steam train to Newcastle where we would do our Christmas shopping. We were given money to purchase presents for one another. With great secrecy we would take them home and wrap them. Mum always came home laden with packages which we helped to carry on the two mile walk along bush tracks to home. The once a year trip to Newcastle was one of great excitement for us, our only other outings were fortnightly shopping trips to Wyong or an occasional trip to Grandma's place in the outer suburbs of Sydney.

A week before Christmas we went in search of a suitable pine tree for a Christmas tree. With a blunt axe I would fell the tree and drag it home. Once home it would be trimmed and dragged in through the doorway and stood into a kerosene tin which was filled with sand. Usually the tree was too big and it would be dragged outside and trimmed some more. This process was repeated until the tree "fit". It was then decorated with all manner of baubles and tinsel paper. Often it would be blown over; our place had doorways but no doors and plenty of holes through which the wind would blow. On Christmas Eve Santa came and mysteriously left presents at the base of the tree. Some of them were similar to the presents we had purchased in Newcastle.

Grandma and Nanna always came to stay at Christmas. Arriving by steam train Dad picked them up in the truck and with us kids sitting on the back we travelled home in great excitement. After the obligatory drink of tea and kisses all round, Nanna took us in search of gum tips and Christmas bells to decorate our home with. These were placed in jars or vases and looked quite a sight.

Christmas morning we are up early to see what Santa had bought during the night. The bottle of beer and cake we had left out was gone and parcels wrapped in brightly coloured paper were arranged around the base of the tree. Presents were ripped open and examined and then we rushed outside to play whilst our parents and grandparents prepared Christmas dinner. Roast pork and vegetables, Christmas pudding with custard, cordial for us and beer for our parents and Grandparents was in order. Nanna always let me have a small glass of beer and when Mum went crook she would say 'it will flush his kidneys out'.

When I grew older I did a fair bit of kidney flushing. When the food was being dished up our job was to 'shoo the flies away and keep our thieving cats at bay'.

Old Mr Flarey was always invited around for Christmas dinner. He regaled us with and stories whilst we ate. When asked 'would you like a drink' he said 'just a small one please'. I noticed he drank numerous "small ones".

Time came for the Christmas pudding. Mum dished up and ensured that everyone got a silver coin in their plate, a sixpence or three pence. We all found ours and waited for Mr Flarey to find his coin. He finished his pudding and no coin. Mum swore she had placed a coin in every plate.

I wonder what happened to Mr Flarey's coin.

The Figure in the White Shirt

They were in love. Two young people. Mary Cassidy and Robert Brown. However, there was a problem. Mary was an Irish Catholic, or at least her parents, Seamus and Anne Cassidy were, and Robert was of English stock, and Protestant.

Staunch Catholics, Seamus Cassidy and his future wife had been transported to the colony as convicts. They met and once they obtained their Certificates of Freedom, took up a small selection along the south bank of an ephemeral stream that flowed (after rain) and eventually joined a large river, the Hawkesbury. There they married and Mary, their first child, was born a year later. Old Seamus Cassidy swore that his eldest daughter Mary was to have nothing to do with that thieving protestant Brown family or their son Robert.

Bigotry was alive and well in the new colony.

By day, Mary helped out on the selection—feeding pigs and fowls, bucket feeding poddy calves with milk she had stripped from the cows or chipping weeds from rows of corn and pumpkins. She also helped her mother with the little ones, she had ten younger siblings and she was just seventeen. Her mother would have one on her hip, one on her breast and usually one in her belly. People would say 'Old Seamus is a randy old bugger!' and the women would say, 'I don't know how she does it'. And she wouldn't have managed without the help of Mary.

The Brown's selection was on the other side of the creek, about three miles distant from Cassidy's farm. There Rueben and his two sons grew corn, barley and pumpkins which they sold to the Government stores or kept as feed for their pigs, cattle and horses. His three daughters helped their mother Ann around the house.

Robert's grandfather, Henry, had been transported to the colony in irons, he had been caught stealing sheep in the old country and was lucky to escape hanging. His grandmother had followed her convict husband out to the colony bringing three children, including Robert's father, Rueben. There she took up a selection and had her husband Henry assigned to her as a servant. Their eldest son Rueben, when he came of age, married, took up land of his own and started a family.

On rare occasions Rueben and his family attended social gatherings, a dance in the church hall, weddings, christenings or funerals. If the Cassidys were present, which they often were, the Browns kept away from them, leaving Robert and Mary to cast furtive glances at each other or signal one another with discreet hand gestures. They strived to sneak away from their ever-watchful families and once together Robert would whispered, 'I'll meet you down by your sliprails tonight.'

Came dark and Robert waited patiently for his family to go to sleep. He lay on his bed in a room he shared with his younger brother, feigning sleep until he could hear his brother snoring quietly with louder stentorious snores coming from his father in an adjoining room. Walking quietly on bare feet he crept from his room, down the passageway, dodging loose floor boards which would creak, (he knew where they were), and creep silently through the dark toward the lovers' meeting place. His mother, who was a light sleeper, often heard him leave and would smile quietly to herself.

Across the creek, young Mary waited until her family slept, then left silently to join her lover who by now was waiting patiently for her.

After a longing embrace they lay together on a blanket Robert had carried with him. The blanket had been hidden in his father's barn and bought out for their clandestine meetings. Soft murmurings could be heard as the lovers embraced in the dark.

Robert's body stiffened! Mary sensed this, 'what's wrong?' she exclaimed. 'Look,' Robert replied, 'someone's there'. He pointed to where a figure wearing a white shirt could be seen, watching them through the gloom. 'Who's that?' Robert croaked, 'who is it?'

Robert and Mary sat up and quickly and rearranged their clothing. Their hearts were pounding with fear.

With a snort, a baldy-faced draft horse turned away and slowly ambled off across the paddock.

The Great Australian Shed

In Australia there are a number of iconic buildings and structures, including the Sydney Opera House, Sydney Harbour Bridge and a number of churches and town halls.

Australian sheds are equally iconic and represent a way of life unique to this country. Our sheds have many forms ranging from hay sheds, farm sheds, chook sheds, backyard sheds. Then there are woolsheds, (also known as shearing sheds) where sheep are fleeced. And, of course, there is that big shed in Canberra, Parliament House, from where the population is fleeced.

A lot towns and suburbs have "Men's Sheds" where old codgers and sometimes younger codgers gather to while away their time; fixing old pushbikes and toys to sell. In these sheds, men can yarn, talk about their female partners and generally escape the humdrum of domestic life. Men's Sheds are the male equivalent of the Country Womens Association (CWA) sometimes referred to by Men's Shed members as the Cranky Womens Association, but never in the presence of their female partners.

In the past sheds were built from whatever materials were readily available. Posts were cut and carried or snigged into place. White mahogany made the best posts. It was reasonably termite resistant and long lasting in the ground. However white mahogany was not available everywhere and then any straight durable timber was used.

After the site was cleared and levelled and the shed parameters pegged out, holes were dug at least three feet (one metre) deep and the posts placed and squared up. This takes what we Aussies call hard yakka. The holes are dug using a bar and shovel. After the posts were stood and secured in place with braces, the holes were back filled and the earth around the posts rammed tight.

Much of this hard graft is still done today in the building of sheds. The posts were cut for height and cross members, also bush poles, wired or bolted to them. Often the cross members would be squared using a broad axe and adze.

Rafters also obtained from the bush would be placed at regular intervals along the cross members and the roofing material would be fixed to these. In the early days corrugated iron was not always available so sheets of bark from Eucalypts known as Stringybark trees were used.

Bark sheets would be cut from the tree and placed over a fire so it could be straightened, then placed on the rafters where it was held down with nails or twitches of wire. If these were not available large rocks would be placed on the bark to hold it down. These are sometimes referred to as Queensland nails. The walls of the shed would be clad with corrugated iron if it was available, bark, or often timber slabs cut and trimmed from suitable logs.

The floor would generally be a dirt floor, but if the shed was to be used as living quarters a mixture of sand and cow dung would be spread over it and compacted. If the shed was fully enclosed a doorway was left open and sometimes shutters built to cover window openings. As the settler became more prosperous the bark roof was replaced with corrugated iron.

In the early days of settlement corrugated iron came from England by steamer or sailing ship and was landed in ports such as Adelaide, Melbourne or Sydney.

It was then transported overland on drays pulled by horse or bullock teams or sometimes carried up inland river systems on paddle steamers. A lot of materials were carried by paddle steamer up the Murray/Darling river system this way and landed at river ports including Wentworth, Menindee, Wilcannia and Bourke. The materials were then carried overland on dray or wagon to their destination. The corrugated iron of that time was far superior to that which is sold today and over one hundred years later is still in use and in good condition. No doubt the dry climate helps preserve it.

A significant number of sheds built in the mid 1800s are still standing. However for some the ravages of wind and rain have spelled their demise and they stand derelict and empty as iron from walls and roofs is scattered across paddocks whenever the wind blows.

Today modern sheds are supplied in kit form and comprise steel framing with painted metal sheets for the walls and ceilings. They are generally erected on a concrete slab.

Most backyards sport a shed of some sort used to store lawn mowers and other garden implements and tools. Some of the larger structures are called "man caves" and are equipped with a bar, television sets, CD players and often a snooker table. They are designed so the "man" can entertain his mates and watch sport and drink, or otherwise involve himself in "men's business" away from the lady of the house and their children.

Women are permitted but generally find it boring and usually head back to the house where they involve themselves with "women's business".

So the evolution of Australia can be seen in the changing style of its sheds over the past two hundred or so years. But nothing beats the romance of a shed, standing in a paddock, often with sheets of iron missing from its walls or roof, or collapsed into an historical ruin on the ground. Visions of the activities that occurred within its walls still evoke memories of the past.

George Townsend

Fishin'

Some folk fish with line and hook, some folk use a sinker,
Sometimes worms are used for bait, sometimes a piece of liver,
Fancy lures, rods and reels, line wound on a bottle,
Full of hope the fisher waits, catch a fish for supper.

I've found a better way to fish; it doesn't take much time,
I don't have to sit and wait; the fish I get are mine,
A little effort, not much work to catch a fish for tea,
I don't have to hold a line; the fish will come to me.

Netting shook from someone's fence, a length of eight gauge wire,
Roll the netting, fit two ends, attach the length of wire,
Make a funnel, fit it tight, tie it to one end,
Find a quiet spot on the river near a steep banked bend.

Fishing's best done on the quiet, don't want anyone to see,
Where the trap is placed in water, fish are just for me,
Sneak down to the bend you've chosen; carefully place your trap,
With the funnel pointing downstream you're sure to get a catch.

Throw the trap into deep water; make sure it's out of sight,
Hide the wire underwater, this is done at night,
Don't leave any tracks to follow, don't leave any sign,
If someone finds your trap -share it, they keep the fish they find.

Once the trap is set you check it every couple of nights,
Just make sure that no one's watching, don't use any lights
Pull it in and take the fish, toss back those too small,
Reset the trap; wipe out your tracks, aint fishing just a ball.

Fishing inspectors lurk about, out to spoil your fun.
If you spot one of these fellows drop your fish and run,
If by chance he sneaks up on you this is what you say,
'Look at this some dirty mongrel; I hope you make him pay.'

Just say the fish trap isn't yours; you found it just by chance,
If you knew the mongrel that set it, by cripes you'd make him dance,
Help the Inspector bust it up, let the fish go free,
And curse this fellow under your breath, no fish for you or me.

George Townsend

Dreams Lonely in the Night

I'm sitting by a fire; stars are shining bright,
A barking owl is calling to his mate out in the night,
Coals are glowing warmly, at them I sit and stare,
And dream of places where I've been, places way out there.

In dreams I visit country towns and travel through the scrub,
Along bitumen or dusty track, or axle deep in mud,
Crossing flooded rivers, facing dust storms in my dreams,
Hear the tyres of a sulky; hear the sound of bullock teams.

I journey through our country, walk along a ferny creek,
I dream the scent of wattle, golden flowers sweet,
I travel through rain forest, down a steep and mossy gorge,
Through sandy scrub and spinifex, cross rivers by the score,

I venture in dark forests where sunlight rarely strikes the ground,
Cross grassy plains and mallee, where kangaroos abound,
Hear the howling of a dingo, curlew screeching out in fright,
Breeze whispering in the gum leaves, emu drumming in the night.

I dream of people that I've met and those I wish I knew,
Blokes like Kelly Dixon who penned a song or two,
Henry Lawson, Ion Idriess both wrote about our land,
Timeless dreaming, heartbreak stories, footsteps in the sand.

Some are gone, I know their tale, I've read of them in books,
Bush battlers, painters, drifters; and scruffy shearer's cooks,
Gold seekers such as Lasseter, a legend in his time,
The Man from Snowy River, Banjo made his story rhyme.

Coals are slowly dimming; night air is getting damp,
Swag unrolled and tucker stowed away from prowling ants,
I hit the sack, lie on my back and gaze into the sky,
And watch the stars move slowly west as the moon begins to rise.

I think of home and loved ones, waiting 'til I return,
I send them wishes on a star; keep them from any harm,
I wonder what they're doing, I wonder if they're right,
I dream that I am with them 'stead of lonely in the night.

George Townsend

Tribal Law

Purposely and quickly he walks across the ground,
Human blood and hair bind emu feathers to his feet,
He stalks the tribal enemy, he never makes a sound,
No tracks are left, no stone disturbed beneath those feathered feet.

A man has broken tribal law, he stole another's wife,
Punishment was passed on him by elders in the night,
His punishment was boning, his sentence was his life,
Kadaitcha was sent to find and put the matters right.

He placed his bag at feathered feet and drew the object out,
Thalta yalku pirna, polished creamy white,
He points the deadly object at his victim who's in sight,
He sends a deadly punishment and hears his victim shout.

Weeks have passed, the victim pines and loses all his will,
His bodies thin, his teeth fall out, he staggers all alone,
Shunned by all who knew him, tribal law is set to kill,
Ritualistic punishment, the pointing of the bone.

Has-beens of the Rodeo

You brag about rodeos across our great wide land,
How someone rode the rankest bull and got the upper hand,
You brag of bulls like Chainsaw, and cowboys that are best,
But what about the has-beens, what about the rest?

Yeah what about the has-beens and the blokes that always bust,
Who've never tasted glory, are always tastin' dust,
Of men that never ride out time, men that never score,
Limping back across the ring, battered bruised and sore.

You talk about rodeo queens and clowns out in the ring,
The men that pull the chute gates, their praises you will sing.
You talk about top cowboys, how judges score their ride,
You talk about rodeos; you talk of them with pride.

Your tales are full of praise for breeders of outstanding cattle,
Of rankest bulls like Dynamite, he always wins the battle,
Of the man behind the microphone, of judges keeping score,
Of how the crowd stood to its feet, of how the crowd did roar.

So while your songs are full of praise for those that are the best,
Just spare a thought for blokes like me that never pass the test,
Who never ride the bulls out, are beaten in the battle,
Who never seem to stick like glue when perched up in the saddle.

So what about the has-beens and the men that always bust,
Who've never tasted glory, are always tastin' dust,
Of men that never ride out time, of men that never score,
Limping back across the ring, battered bruised and sore.

George Townsend

Rusty iron... worn out dingo traps

I scrounged around the station tip to see what I could find,
Amongst broken bottles, worn out traps and rusty roofing iron,
Old sulky wheels and bits of steel, a broken cobblers last,
Memories were before me, memories of the past.

I gazed at all this worn out gear from days that are long gone,
At bells and harness, leather hard, and buckles that once shone.
Before TV stars and motor cars, international wars and strife,
Of days that's gone before my time, memories of a past life.

I wonder at this broken wheel, if it could talk I'd know,
Its travels through our great wide land, places that I'd go,
Down dusty track or bogged in mud, crossing flooded streams,
Wayside shanties, old bush pubs, a lot of life it's seen.

A rusted dog trap has a tale I'm sure that it would tell,
Of how the wild dog mauled the sheep, the trap was set to kill,
Its jaws wrapped with strychnine cloth, placed where wild dogs came,
It served a useful purpose, 'twas set to kill or maim.

This coil of rusted wire once strung out across the flat,
Confining sheep to blue bush plains to sell when they were fat.
A pile of broken bottles, once full of cooling beer,
End of shearing, cut out party, shearers full of cheer.

An old 'T' model once brand new, its paint has rusted off,
The pride of this large station, carried squatter and the toff.
Later models sitting idle amongst the tins and jars,
Tell the story of the station evolving through its cars.

Lying here, amongst the tins, a broken cobblers last,
When boots were mended, not thrown out, old practice from the past,
A pile of worn out horseshoes, a broken bullock bell,
Made by the station smithy, oh what tales they'd tell.

So the story of this station is set out for you to see,
Every item has a story just for you and me.
Much more value than scrap metal, fills up histories gaps,
Rusty iron and broken bottles, worn out dingo traps.

George Townsend

Toyota Dreaming

Ancestral beings, rainbow snakes are sung about at night,
Dancers painted, sacred markings gleam in fire light,
Rhythmic clapping, dancers stamping, droning didgeridoo,
People singing, elders chanting, roasting kangaroo.
Generations told these stories, dreaming kept alive,
Ceremony, rituals practiced, taught to all the tribe,
Culture vibrant, eyes excited, landscape features form,
Stories told of earths creation, taught from dusk to dawn.

Invasion of this wide brown country, dreaming starts to fade,
Land is stolen, rights are taken, taken right away,
Repressed people, condemned to silence, not allowed to speak,
Mission captives, fed on handouts, life is made so cheap.
Enlightened government, Native Title, Reconciliation push,
Multi Nationals, new invasion, their quest to clear the bush,
Compensation from the miners, dollars given out,
Toyota Dreaming, lots of money, excited people shout.

What's the price of generations, dreaming stories told,
Destroy a country for some money, paid with bribery gold,
Traditional Dreaming is now fading, Toyota Dreaming now,
Age old culture led to slaughter, like a fatted cow.
People see no more than dollar, see what they can buy,
Cars and TV's, video players, watch the money fly,
Dollars blinding, lack of vision, old dreamings soon are lost,
New found dreaming, Toyota Dreaming, culture is its cost.

Tony Lang

Tony Lang OAM is a retired Army chaplain who lives on the shores of Lake Macquarie with his wife Janet and their two "children" Tonkie (cat) and Jock (dog). He has written six books; four under the pseudonym of "Lachlan Ness" and two children's books under his own name. A third children's book is on the way. Tony has had parishes in NSW and Qld, Shetland and mainland Scotland.

Young Love, First Love

Who cannot remember their first romantic love? 'Way back in the 50's there was a song that said it all, and that song was: *Young Love, First Love*. Usually it's the first love of our lives that we never forget, for whatever reason. It's rare for the first love to be the last love. The road from first love to last love is generally littered with numerous potholes and dead ends.

I've never forgotten the time I met my first love. She was so gorgeous. It was back in the town of Leeton, NSW, 'Heart of the MIA' and if you don't know what that stands for, it's 'Murrumbidgee Irrigation Area'. Great rice-growing area. We also used to grow the most beautiful peaches, oranges, apricots, tomatoes and other fruits and vegetables, most of which made their way to 'Letona': Leeton Cooperative Cannery, now sadly no more. More importantly, we also produced the most beautiful girls. They probably still do, down there, not far from the gently flowing waters of the beautiful 'bidgee. I'm not sure why the girls were so lovely… could have been the channel water that we all drank and swam in, or the quality of what grew on our vines and fruit trees, or it could have been the fact that in those days people didn't travel as widely as they do today, so we couldn't compare them as readily, but whatever the reason, all the Leeton girls were naturally attractive. After such an introduction to the superb quality of the Leeton girls, it seems strange to commence with a story of my first love: a girl who wasn't Leeton-born.

You can read this as a 'true confession' if you like, for I've never forgotten her. I recall the first time I saw her. It was love at first sight… love 'across a crowded room', literally. We belonged to the same organization so I saw her only Monday to Friday. I didn't have a car; only a pushbike, and I don't think she was the type who'd have enjoyed being 'dinked' on a pushbike!

On the day I first saw her she was talking to someone who faded into insignificance in her presence. She turned slightly and caught me, staring at her with unbridled admiration. Instead of ignoring me, she threw me a radiant smile that almost obliterated me. I think my heart stopped. In the warmth of that smile I saw a promise of things to come. I wasn't just one of a number in that room of milling people that day in late summer – her smile made me ten feet tall!

Her figure was so elegant, her movements graceful as a swan's. She wore a pale-blue twin-set with a white blouse, and it suited her slender figure perfectly. Each time she turned her head, the sunlight streaming through the window highlighted the beauty of her nutbrown hair that framed her sweet face. Even the sun seemed besotted as it hovered its beams around her, highlighting a little tint here and there, or resting gently and too briefly on her face, appearing reluctant to move from her. Her name was Heather…. such a pretty name.

There's no doubt about it – I fell in love with her immediately and completely. It wasn't simply the fact that she was very pretty. There was an aura of calm and gentleness around her. I decided I had to make her mine; to court her, gently. I saw her almost daily. I thought at first she may have been rather shy, noting that she'd bring a sandwich to lunch, sit by herself and read. One day, by a strange 'coincidence' I was there too. At first she seemed to prefer to ignore me as we sat eating our lunch. Slowly, however, I won her over, and we'd spend lunch time talking over all sorts of things; mostly associated with work, for she held a position senior to mine.

One day as she stood to return to her office, I, greatly daring, slipped my hand into hers. In a time when there was such a thing as propriety,

I half-expected her to withdraw hers. She didn't –she gave my hand a little squeeze! Oh – boundless bliss! We walked hand in hand to her office where regretfully I released her. In the face of such encouragement, my initial hesitation turned to recklessness. I decided to hasten proceedings and ask her to marry me.

The opportunity presented itself a few months later – a 'now or never' moment; a time when we can speak or forever hold our peace. This was the time. As she stood to go back to her office, I took her hands in mine. 'Heather, would you… will you… marry me?' I knew my face was the colour of tomato soup, and my voice to my ears sounded like a radio off its station – a hideous crackle I barely recognised. I saw at once I'd taken her completely by surprise. She withdrew her hands and smiled; a sad smile, a compassionate smile – a rejecting smile. My heart began to break. I couldn't understand it… all that time; time when I was certain I'd won her heart, had been for nothing. In that one sad yet compassionate smile, I knew it was all over.

'Tony dear, you're the first who has ever asked me, and it hurts me deeply to tell you that I can't ma - '

'Why can't you marry me? I thought you loved me!' Real men don't cry, but I couldn't help it. My shattered heart released the waters of Burrinjuck. Quietly she slipped me her handkerchief.

As I took it, her hand closed over mine in a loving, understanding, comforting way. I knew that she still cared for me, even if it wasn't in the way I so desperately wanted it to be.

'I do love you, Tony dear, but it's a different sort of love. Romantic love cannot exist between us. I'm twenty-two, and you're only six. I'm your teacher. I love all of you.' She gestured to the class.

She left at the end of that year. It took me a long time to recover – probably all of six months.

Years later, I met Heather H again. She was 92 and still retained something of her former loveliness and all her sweet nature. She never married – something that baffles me to this day.

Privations of an Army Padre

The padre, wartime or peacetime, is expected to be able to do what all the troops do. This following is taken from a diary extract from my time as a chaplain with the Australian Regular Army. It details a navigation exercise through the Cooloola State Forest in Qld.

I set off with my section one fine morning, loaded with packs and webbing, bound for Poona Lake, a little freshwater lake deep in the rainforest. It was once the habitat of an Aboriginal tribe that had lived there for centuries. Within ten years of the white man's coming, they were all gone—many shot, the survivors fled, as the history is told.

The going was not particularly easy. It seemed to be almost all uphill. Finally, however, we arrived. It seems not many people visit Poona Lake. It is small and ringed by reeds. Over the years falling leaves have turned the water to the colour of tea, but it's fresh and drinkable. We set up camp, lit a fire, brewed up our tucker, then sat around yarning, as soldiers will.

A strange aura hangs over the place ... we almost spoke in whispers. When looking for somewhere to throw my sleeping bag, I'd followed a narrow track through the reeds. At the end was a 'wallaby lay'—a circular, flattened area of reeds where the animals camp at night. I settled comfortably into my reedy bed, with the waters of the lake lapping a short distance away. A strong wind had sprung up, and in the darkness above stars twinkled, then disappeared behind scudding cloud. I could see the silhouettes of tall reeds and trees waving about me. The brooding nature of the place had affected us all, more or less, and was even more pronounced in the solitude.

My thoughts returned to that long-dead tribe. In the darkness I could almost sense their presence, gazing at me with sad eyes. I've slept in many outlandish places over the years, but none has affected me quite like Poona Lake. It is an eerie place, yet strangely peaceful, in a sad and lonely way.

Further up the rise, the rest of the section were having their own problems. They had come to the attention of the local bush rats, who welcomed them with open paws. Through the night the rodents scurried busily about, breaking into the odd ration pack, enjoying survival biscuits, chocolate, sugar. The occasional shine of a torch revealed beady little eyes, set in cheeky little faces, staring back curiously, happy to share their humble lodgings for a morsel of food. One venturesome little beastie even sampled some hair. The scream of the sleeping owner who awoke *very* suddenly was probably heard back at base camp…

Next morning early we were away again. The going was even harder—upwards we climbed, into the beautiful heart of the rainforest.

Ancient trees, with huge moss-covered, gnarled trunks soared into the sky, forming a leafy canopy thirty metres above us. Strange, tropical flowers bloomed among the dense green of the forest and massive staghorns spilled from trees fifteen metres above us. Creepers as thick as a man's arm twined about trees while our soldiers' boots brushed through delicate fernery. Heavy bush impeded our way, making the going very hard indeed.

We navigated our way to the coast and made our camp on a hill near the beach. We rested and prepared our evening meal from dwindling rations, then gazed out on a purpling sea.

Up the coast we could see light flashing from Double Island Point Lighthouse, while on the seaward horizon there were fitful flashes of lightning as a thunderstorm rumbled and grumbled its way across the bosom of the deep. We were too tired to erect our hoochies* and lay where we fell…

At 0200 I awoke. Rain was pelting down. The startled faces of the men were revealed in a brilliant flash of lightning. Clad only in underdacks I jumped out of my sleeping bag and secured my hoochy to some nearby bushes. To be caught in the open in a thunderstorm is an unhappy experience, tingled with fear ("one flash and you're ash" is a distinct possibility).

Thankfully we survived until daylight arrived. I discovered that my shirt, unlike the rest of my gear, was suffering from cold and exposure. There are few objects clammier than a shirt, already stiff with a couple of days' sweat and grime, which is sopping wet and must be donned at 0600!

Later that day we marched back into base camp, after many kilometres of rugged and wildly beautiful country. From there we went in trucks back to our units on the Base, a few hundred kilometres way.

Back home again, in our married quarters on the Base, I am strangely restless. The bed is too soft and comfortable. I'm tempted to grab my sleeping bag and sleep on the lawn. China cups have a funny feel on the lips after the comforting heat of a blackened tin mug, and there is no sand in my tea. I miss my own kfs and tin Dixie. At night, I cannot see the stars in the ceaseless rim along the edge of eternity, nor scudding clouds across a yellow moon.

No shy bush creatures peer at me curiously from mysterious haunts deep in the bush, and neither wind nor wave lulls me into physically exhausted sleep…

Oh well, such is civilization; but do you ever have that niggling feeling deep in the inner recesses of your mind that 'civilization' may not be all that it's cracked up to be?

(*a *hoochy is a canvas shelter, a little longer and slightly wider than the average body, with no sides, that ties onto handy shrubs etc.*)

The Magic Mist

I strolled into the bush one day -
What happened next is hard to say.
A fairy-mist the forest wreathed
And charmed the very air I breathed.
A magic aura touched each tree,
Each plant and creature – even me.
Beyond the normal world I knew,
A hidden earth had come to view.
Across my path marched lines of ants
In brightly coloured shoes and pants.

I knew that in the misty haze
Stranger sights would meet my gaze.
The next I saw – I swear it's true:
A bush hat on a kangaroo!
He gave a wave and smiled at me
(And that was odd enough to see),
But stranger still, I must relate,
He spoke to me: 'How are you, mate?'
Then doffed his hat with practised ease
And bounded off among the trees.

I shook my head – my mind was numb.
I wondered what was yet to come.
And then before my very eyes
I had another great surprise.
Along a track I'd wandered down
A wombat in a dressing gown
Sat drinking tea and eating toast.
'Come, sit,' he said, 'I'll be your host.'
He nodded to his table there
And to another, vacant chair.
I sat at once. The chair was small,
For wombats are not very tall.
We chatted on of this and that,
I spoke in English, he, Wombat.

And when at last I rose to go,
He waved the teapot to and fro.
'Just one more round of toast and tea
And then we can part company.'
He shook my hand, I took his paw,
Then stayed another hour or more.

I wandered on, till wearied sank
On a billabong's grassy bank.
Just then I heard a gentle song
That floated from the billabong.
I was entranced! A golden carp
Sat playing on an Irish harp,
A sweet and mystic melody
Of life beneath her inland sea.
Cumbungi swayed and sang along
By that enchanted billabong.

'The song is lovely! I could stay
And listen to it all the day!'
I called to her. She heard it clear,
For in her eye I saw a tear.
'I can but stay for just a minute;
My air must have some water in it,
So take a willow, soft and fine,
And with it soothe my golden spine.
I do this every thousand years,
For weeping willows hold my tears.'

I turned, and there upon the shore
A weeping willow tree I saw.
I took a branch, as I was told,
And with it soothed her spine of gold.
She sighed. 'Your kindness I'll not spurn;
I'll give you something in return.'
Then she was gone! The waters bland
Had swallowed her, but in my hand,

When I my fingers did uncurl,
Found there a lovely, golden pearl.

I wandered from that magic place
With slow and steady, lingering pace,
And every creature that I viewed
Was full of colour, brightly hued.
Birds flew round on silvered wing,
While bees could talk and trees could sing.
But suddenly, before my gaze
That world was gone; so was the haze.
The mystic place that I'd been shown
Was now the bush I'd always known.

Long years have passed, yet still I yearn
To see that magic world's return.
And on the bushland paths, always
I hope to see the mystic haze.
I saw a 'roo one day, and think
He passed me with a knowing wink.
Sometimes I wonder if I'm mad
Or if it was a dream I had,
But when those doubts begin to swirl,
I gaze upon my golden pearl.

The story behind the Magic Mist: For over twenty years I served as a police chaplain both in Central Qld and NSW. Those years produced many adventures; some exciting, some funny and of course many sad. On one of those occasions I was called out to assist police and volunteers as they searched for a man who had vanished in dense bush. It seems that had driven to a spot nearby and gone for a walk from which he never returned and in fact was never found. I was told a strange note had been found in the car and that was the catalyst that started the book, 'The Magic Mist' and its sequel, 'An Australian Bush Fantasy'.
*(The poem, The Magic Mist has been published as a children's book of the same name and is available on Amazon. The sequel is in another children's book, 'An Australian Bush Fantasy')

The Day an APC* Flew

A tale told by a pilot in the officers' mess, at the Army Aviation Centre, Oakey, Qld.

The major had a tale to tell; he called the pilots round:
'Stick to the air, it's safer there, than on the flamin' ground!'
This is the story that he told (his name must not be aired)
Of how he flew an APC, and this is how he fared.

It happened at a training ground, to soldiers quite well known,
The only time on record that an APC has flown.
I was sitting on an APC, being driven down the track,
And as I watched the driver, I thought I'd like a crack.
He must have read my mind, for he offered with a smile,
To fulfil my great ambition of driving for a while.

I got into the driver's seat and did as I was told,
And soon I had the hang of it – I went as good as gold.
Rudder left – rudder right – 'It handles like a tank!'
'It should!' the nervous driver said. Well, that explained the clank.
'Turn left!' the driver said again. I turned with all my might,
But something must have happened, for the ruddy thing went right.
I gunned the mighty engine, to show it who was boss,
But to explain what happened then, I'm really at a loss.

I'm sure we reached our take-off speed, we travelled so swift,
So I pulled back on the joystick, to give the thing some lift.
The driver screamed his head off, as we became unstuck,
But not for long (the trim was wrong)—we landed with a 'gluck.'
Yes, we'd landed in a sea of mud, and it began to creep
Further up, right past the tracks; it really was quite deep.
I confess it really worried me; it's not the way I'd choose
To depart this pleasant world of ours, beneath that muddy ooze.

'If I lose my life, I'll be in strife,' the driver said to me,
'For I won't be there at all to sign the QM's L&D.'*
Just then on shore with joy we saw a welcome little band
Who'd come to help at last. It seemed that rescue was at hand.

On Terra Firma's solid soil at last we were pulled free,
But how that thing got in the air remains a mystery.
So pilots all just heed my call: low flying in the fog
Is nowhere near as dangerous as landing in a bog.

The heavier the thing you fly, the more it puts to test
What happens when you land it. A butterfly lands best.
I'd much prefer to fly, propellered and with wings,
Than with turret and with tracks and other heavy things.

Just buy another round boys, you've heard it all from me
Of how I tried (I nearly died!) to fly an APC!'

                Chaplain (Major) Tony Lang (Ret'd).

*APC: Armoured Personnel Carrier.
*QM: Quartermaster
*L&D: Loss and Damage report

Dream Sheep

When Jock our dog is sleeping on his comfy bed at night,
I know when he's not 'with me' though in my line of sight.
He gives a little twitch and yelp, upon his palliasse
And I'm sure he's chasing dream sheep on a farm just out of Yass.
Jock's a border collie and for chasing sheep was bred,
And though it's in his very blood it somehow missed his head.
The farmer pointed to our boy: 'You just don't have the knack,
It grieves me much to say it Jock – I'm giving you the sack.'

'When I give you a sharp command, I don't know why I bother.
It seems to enter in one ear, and straight out through the other.
Your long-term memory I'm sure would never win a prize;
I rather think a matchstick head would be about its size.'
None of this I knew of course, for I don't live out there,
But it came to the attention of a Vet I know, called Claire.
When she heard that Jock was sacked, she went out to the farm
And brought him back with her, in case he came to any harm.

Now Jock has come to live with us and is our special joy,
Although I'll tell you freely that he's not a morning boy.
He finds his bed just to his taste and on it likes to lie,
And does not like to stir until the sun's well in the sky.
Jock's a faithful, loving boy; a gentle, happy friend;
He's happy most when with us, from morn till evening's end.
Those qualities come first for us; they're in his spirit deep,
So we really are quite happy that he failed in chasing sheep.

And when I think about our boy, there is another side:
The sheepdog breed is in his blood and will not be denied.
He's with his siblings in his dreams, Bonnie, Lad and Lass,
Rounding up the dream sheep on that farm just out of Yass.

My Prostate Op

I will tell you of the fate of my rebellious old prostate
Which brought me endless strife and ceaseless woe.
I was fit as I could be, for each night I had to pee
A dozen times, so walked a mile or so.

Said Jen my little wife, 'you've had enough of strife,
So with the doc I'll make an a-ppoint-ment.
You'll have to keep it though; if you're too afraid to go,
You'll have ME to deal with.' So of course I went.

The doctor had a prod and said 'You poor old sod,
Your waterworks are gummed up down below.
Now I will have to yield to an expert in that field.
I'll call a handy plumber that I know.'

And so a few weeks later I was sent off to the Mater
(The hospital – the best they say, by far).
It really made me blush where they used that shaving brush
But my underdacks now cover up the scar.

Yes, the plumber did the job; I know his name is Bob,
He left me feeling stiff and rather sore,
But he was good and he was fast, and I knew the job would last:
He'd fixed our 'loo a year or so before.

'You won't have cause to gripe, I used good copper pipe,
At soldering I am the very best;
So when you want to pee, pull that bathplug in your knee,
And turn the tap that's soldered to your chest.'

I did recuperate from that painful old prostate,
I sleep all night and never leave the sack.
For that I have to thank the fifty litre tank
That Bob has kindly soldered to my back.

As for volume, you should see just how high that I can pee!
The Sydney Harbour Bridge I think I'd clear.
The secret is the pump that bolted to my rump
And wired to that switch beside my ear.

So if walking down the street one day you chance to meet
A walking hardware store, why then you'll know
Although I look a mess, my op. was a success,
And Bob the plumber is the way to go.

The Spider Queen

Last night I saw her,
Regally pale in the glow of the moon.
Her dress, a gown of silk,
Ornate with dew, like fairy pearls,
Was spread about her; her coronet
A crown of distant stars.
Her beauty caught my breath while she,
Unmoved, uncaring as a queen
Hung in the silver night on delicate feet.
I wonder if she, curled in her leafy throne
Through the long, sleepy day,
Remembers the glow of the moon's caress,
Remembers her sparkling, sequined dress
(tied with silk to the sentinel trees);
Remembers the song in the cool dawn breeze?

Al Mewett

Al Mewett is like the man who leapt on his horse and went in four directions at once. He took up Theological studies in 1952 and enjoyed a successful ministry for over 25 years. Al took on retail management with Grace Bros, Sports Management, then Real Estate & Property Development with a little government lobbying on the side. Al retired in Newcastle. Now the horse is stabled, perhaps another book can find its way to our shelves.

Sitting in Bligh's Chair

The impeccably dressed waiter stood behind me. The Governor of Tasmania, sitting beside me had just been served with strawberries and cream in a silver sweet dish emblazoned with the State Crest. Now it was my turn. My turn to be the centre of a major crisis. The silver dish clipped my shoulder and tumbled down my arm. Two bounces on the sleeve of my dark green jacket ensured the contents had been well spread.

The Governor looked askance. If it wasn't the greatest tragedy to have unfolded in the Tasmanian Government House, it was certainly the most recent.

I feel you will not be satisfied until I reveal just what we were doing in such a prestigious venue, so we shall put that right and get on with the story. The Bowls Australia Championships were being held in Hobart which meant the governing body comprising representatives from each state and territory was in attendance. And why wouldn't they be? Their travel and accommodation together with all meals and hospitality were all paid for from club subsidies. To this day I can't understand why they needed two from each state. Still, it's only money.

The Governor of Tasmania was pleased to give us a Civic reception, welcoming bowlers from all over Australia, but for the officials (we can't do without them) he hosted a special dinner. This worried me a little. Not all members of the board were well versed in protocol. Indeed, bowlers per se seem to have a change of personality when events like High Tea come their way. They seem to swarm over the tables and make short work of what is on offer. One theatre in Glenbrook NSW, featured a comedy based on bowls and for an extra fee, patrons could share in a specially prepared "nosh up." By the time many of the patrons had arrived they found that the bowlers had beaten them to it. It's a bowls thing. (Never did get back my fee).

To ensure correct protocol was observed I called the board members together to run down a few do's and don'ts; things such as there will be a seating plan at the entrance of the banqueting hall. Look for your name ... no one will show you to your seat. Do not sit before the Governor is seated and do not commence eating until the Governor has begun. This mini-lecture was not well received by all. "Who is he to tell us what to do?"

Well, the time came and the confusion began. Forget the seating plan. The guy who did it obviously didn't know that Harry wanted to sit next to Jack and on it went. Meals were being served and the Governor graciously waited until all guests had been attended to. Right opposite the Governor was a very hungry board member. He was three mouthfuls ahead of the host and going strong. When it came to dessert, I took centre stage with my decorated jacket. Before I could assure the Governor the people of Tasmania would not be responsible for dry cleaning, one board member had pushed back his chair and proceeded to retrieve my dish. I pleaded with him as I lifted the table cloth, "Let it be, leave it."

The Governor looked as though he could not believe what was happening. He looked me square in the face and raised his eyebrows as though seeking some explanation. Then came the crisis. In reply to my pleading to "Let it go," the voice from under the table let out a triumphant cry, "I can get it!" He was as good as his word; he emerged from under the table, pushed back the white table cloth and held up the dish. The astonished waiter relieved him of his trophy.

In a quiet moment relaxing with drinks (unspilled), the Governor gave me the surprising news that I had been sitting where Governor

Bligh had sat. "You don't mean Captain Bligh of Mutiny of the Bounty fame, do you, Your Excellency?"

"The same," he said. "You sat in his chair at this very table." How on earth did Captain Bligh end up in Tasmania? I just had to know.

On 28th April, 1789, Fletcher Christian led a mutiny against Captain Bligh. The sailors had enjoyed a utopian life in Tahiti and were not happy to leave the beautiful native girls. Then there was the problem of the harsh punishments given so freely by Captain Bligh, and Fletcher Christian had the numbers.

Eighteen loyal to Bligh were sent away in a seven metre open boat equipped with a quadrant and a pocket watch. No chart or compass was made available to them. The mutineers settled on Pitcairn Island and burned the Bounty. Bligh is famous for his brilliant seamanship, he brought his men home to England safe and well. After the hearing the government sent HMS Pandora to go after the mutineers.

The Pandora reached Tahiti on 25th March 1791. Four of the mutineers gave themselves up immediately while another ten were arrested a few weeks later. On the return trip HMS Pandora ran aground on the Great Barrier Reef with a loss of 31 crew and 4 prisoners. Finally. Back in England the Naval Board hanged three mutineers, acquitted four and pardoned three.

The outer western suburbs of Sydney takes in a suburb named Minchinbury. It is after Prospect and before St Marys. In 1808 the opposition against the Governor Bligh was so great that Major George Johnson called the troops to arms and imposed Martial Law. Governor Bligh had beaten one mutiny at sea and been sent to New South Wales as Governor. He now had a mutiny on land. The leading citizens of Sydney demanded Major Johnson arrest Governor Bligh. The military regiment marched to Government House whilst liquor flowed to soldiers and civilians alike.

There were scenes of riot and insubordination everywhere. A watercolour in the Mitchell Library shows Governor Bligh hiding under a bed and being dragged out by Corporal Minchin. For his part, the good corporal was given a grant of land at Minchin. The suburb now rejoices in the name of Minchinbury. For a long time vineyards were the mainstay of Minchinbury. Governor Bligh denied he was hiding under a bed. He claimed he was hiding important documents.

Anyone reading the story of Bligh would believe him. He was afraid of no man. What was not generally known is that before he took up duties as Governor of NSW, he commanded HMS Glatton, under the command of Admiral Nelson who admired his ability. It was Sir Joseph Banks who recommended Bligh for Governor of NSW. In the words of Banks, "He is a man who would brook no nonsense."

Lieutenant Colonel Patterson assumed the Governorship in 1809, authorising Bligh to leave for England. Instead Bligh headed for Tasmania and moved into Government House, Hobart, and stayed there for nine months. Now I know why I sat in his chair and dined at his table.

Britain now realised that the colony had grown to such an extent that it was beyond the power of a naval officer to administer. From this point on military officers were to be the Governors. Lieutenant Colonel Lachlan Macquarie was forty eight years old, a fine officer and a Christian gentleman.

This did not go down well with those who mocked the Christian religion. Macquarie had instructions from England to restore Bligh to power for one day before officially taking command. It was New Year's Day 1810 that Lachlan Macquarie addressed soldiers and civilian alike, calling for an end of dissention, asking for a spirit of reconciliation between all classes of society.

Almost twenty years after Macquarie's reforms, Roger Therry, an Irish lawyer arrived in Sydney, full of praise for what had been achieved. He noted that Sydney did not look like a penal capital. He noted the cleanliness of the wide, well laid out streets, the houses built in the English style, shops well stocked, even jewellers' shops. English roses were growing on verandahs and a nice touch was the regimental bands playing as the sun set. Lachlan Macquarie had made a vibrant city.

Therry's evaluation soon met the light of day when the gates of the convict prison opened, allowing hundreds of convicts to march out on their way to the many public work sites. They were yoked to wagons filled with stone and gravel. Back home in England those labours would have been performed by horses. It was not unusual for twenty men each day to be marched into Hyde Park Barracks to be flogged. Passersby heard the screams.

By the late 1820s the Bushrangers had made their presence felt. Any farmer or businessman with a loaded dray was a target. The bushrangers emerged from the bush, relieved the driver of his valuable load and disappeared. The roads from Tenterfield to the Illawarra were fertile hunting grounds.

It was at this time that 'Bold' Jack Donahoe became our first Wild Colonial Boy and a local hero of the convict population.

Governor Darling introduced the Bushranging Act to fight this new wave of lawlessness. A convicted bushranger would be executed within a day or two of his arrest. Joining this band was the first Chinese bushranger, Sam Poo. Taking goods from Australia by the Chinese has now become quite legal as many ships each day filled with Australian coal sail to Chinese ports.

The elite in the crime world in England were the safe crackers. One especially has been immortalised as 'Sudden Solomon' who, for the good of England, was shipped to Botany Bay.

George Blackston walked the streets of Sydney as a free man, no one knows quite why, but his lifestyle would ensure he would be looking through iron bars in the not too distant future.

George stumbled over a grating in Lower George Street and relieved his tension with a good spray of superlatives. Being a professional he noted a large drainage tunnel and followed its course to potential wealth. It ran just under the foundations of the Bank of Australia.

This bank was not popular with Sydneysiders as it had been formed by the sheep breeder John Macarthur and his elite friends in opposition to The People's Bank of New South Wales.

George had a nose for detail and soon found an ex-convict who had helped build the bank. This man had a mind as clear as bell and was able to supply George with diagrams of the strongroom and drainage tunnels. George recruited his team and Australia's first bank robbery was underway. On 13th September, 1828, the opening was made in the strongroom floor and the men, working away calmly, ransacked the bank. Most of the citizens rejoiced at the news next day. The loot was split seven ways. To have the money returned, the bank offered one hundred pounds reward. (Almost set up a man for life in those days). The Governor chipped in with offer of a free pardon and a return to England. As good as the offer was, the mouths of Sydneysiders were kept well and truly closed.

It all came apart when Sudden Solomon went through his share like a drunken sailor and sought to replenish his fortune by robbing a gambling den. The watchman shot him in the knee. George was sent to Norfolk Island where the constant meeting with the lash broke him. He betrayed his partners in the bank robbery, claimed the pardon trip home to England offered by Governor Darling.

While he was waiting for a ship to England, George attempted to rob a shop and was once again arrested.

The worst was yet to be. It may be seen as poetic justice—George was assigned to a road gang. I know you can see this coming but I'll write it anyway. In the gang were the mates he had "dobbed" in order to qualify for his pardon. You know what happened next too. In 1844 Sudden Solomon was found dead in a swamp.

Grace Bros Australia

It is said that Napoleon's horse once reared and a corporal broke the lines to come to Napoleon's aid, calming the horse. The Emperor shouted, "Thank you, captain." To which the corporal responded, "Of what regiment sir?"

Here was a guy who was not going to miss an opportunity for promotion. For some reason the General Manager of Parramatta Grace Bros. was angered at the administrative personnel and possibly a rush of blood to the brain made him look into my eyes and say, "You're the new store manager." I have never missed a good opportunity to shut up and I could see no point in arguing with him, I simply became the new store manager.

My secretary advised me that a lady on the telephone wanted to thank me for the comedy hit show Are You being Served?

I replied that it was an English comedy, which had nothing to do with the Australian Grace Bros. She knew me well. "Don't tell me, she said; "Tell her."

The lady was effusive. She loved Captain Peacock asking John Inman, "Mr Humphries are you free?" She loved young Mr Grace being supported by two beautiful nurses and secretaries and telling everyone they had all done very well. She thanked me profusely for sponsoring the program and asked me to ensure that the program would not be taken off.

I thanked her for her for taking the time to express her appreciation, and promised that as far as I was concerned it would stay on forever.

Well, that was 1974 still Foxtel is playing "Are You Being Served?" every day of the week. I am a man of my word!

It was the night of an executive dinner at Broadway, Sydney when a colleague took my arm and drew me into the cleaners' room. The aroma was confusing; all those chemicals, mops and cleaning utensils. The room was dimly lit. He looked really excited as he took me by the shoulders and blurted out, "They're sending you to America. I wanted to be the first to tell you."

You can choose your career, your spouse and your hobbies but you can't choose your purpose. Grace Bros had a purpose for me and this included evaluating management and financial procedures in some of America's largest retail operations. I was also to represent the Company at the world national retailers and Merchants Association in New York.

The official announcement was made in one of the Director's offices. It was a more impressive environment, walls lined with books, the smell of leather lounges and an impressive desk. He handed me my itinerary and enough money to make me gasp. However, I can still smell the chemicals in the cleaning room.

Walt Disney was afraid of mice. That did not prevent him from developing an astonishing new world, featuring his favourite character, Mickey Mouse. My study tour began in Los Angeles, visiting the magnificent Disneyland. How this operation guided thousands of visitors to the numerous attractions in an orderly fashion defies belief. I believe it's wasted on children. Any thinking adult stands in amazement at the brilliant management, which keeps it operational. Mickey was there with Donald Duck, as was Snow White with her dwarves. At the end of the day they would take off their heads and go home to the real world. Walt Disney died before Disneyland had opened. One executive, drinking in the success of the opening day remarked, "I wish Walt could have seen this."

Mrs Disney simply replied, "He did, that's why it's here."

It was said to Helen Keller that it was the worst affliction she could have, not having sight. She replied it was worse for those who had sight but no vision. Disney had a vision, which he gave to the world.

Macey's in New York, was the largest department store in the world. The President began our interview with great courtesy, but became more and more agitated as we talked. He could not believe that the Australian shop assistant was given, penalty rates. In the US, if a staff member worked on Saturday and Sunday, she would take off Monday and Tuesday. No penalty rates applied. He was stunned as I explained how long service worked, up to three months off with pay. What really made him thump the desk was the fact that four weeks' leave was given each year together with a seventeen and a half per cent holiday loading.

At that time the statuary holiday in the US was one week per year. Most companies would grant two. Seers Roebuck said if the employee worked well for five years they would be rewarded with a three week vacation. The President was angry, pounding the desk. "I'm the President of the God-damned company and I can't get a four week vacation." He then went on to lecture me as to why the gross national product of the USA was better than that in Australia. We were giving away our profits. As for staff, "Go for a 75% casual rate son, that will get your expenses down." I made a note to give that point priority in my report to the Company.

The New York meeting of the National retail Merchants' Association in New York comprised the most successful businessmen in the country, with the exception of one. The guy from Australia was a greenhorn. The leader advised he had an outstanding training film, featuring John Cleese. It was called "Fear Uncertainty and Doubt "and it would revolutionise sales. He asked how many managers we should have in a store of 100 employees. The Australian voice said "Approximately 50% of the staff." You could have heard a pin drop. "What made you say that, sir?" he asked. "Well, I used that film in

Australia six months ago and it called on staff to mentor co-workers, therefore managing their salesmanship and organisational skills. We became managers rather than mere employees." Someone should have told me that when you are with the Yankees, it is time to shut up. The remainder of the session was very cold indeed. Americans love to talk about their successes; they don't want to hear about yours.

I matured slowly. It didn't concern me however, because Albert Einstein was also a slow learner. That was until I dropped a clanger during the discussion period. "Why doesn't America adopt the metric system?" asked the Australian. All eyes turned to me and I could feel them boring into my soul. "Why should we?" they asked. It was too late now, the train had left the station. "To keep in line with the rest of the world," I limply replied. That did it. My leader shouted at me, "Who needs the God damned rest of the world?"

Would you believe I was on a roll and I couldn't get off. "Well, you need their oil," was my rejoinder. The conference was over for me. I became persona non grata. "Son, we have so much oil in the States, capped and uncapped, we can go by ourselves forever." When I asked why then was it they took oil from the Middle East, all pretence at nicety was over. They shook hands and hoped the company would send another representative next year.

It was so stressful, visiting Niagara Falls, the CNN Tower in Toronto, the Twin Towers building in New York together with sitting in a United Nations meeting, that Grace Bros said I needed a rest on the way home. A hotel was booked on Waikiki Beach. In the surf I stubbed my toes on some rock lava and learned that the beach was built up periodically with sand from Stockton in Newcastle, NSW.

I reported to the Company Secretary on my return and gave him an account of all that I had spent and the money I had left over. He confirmed what the Yanks thought of me. He looked at me as though I was stupid and simply turned away saying, "Go away and do your maths again." The company was not used to dealing with small change.

Back at the desk I decided to cost cut further by sacking our nursing sister who worked on Saturday and Thursday nights. We had a full-time nursing sister because of the thousands visiting our store each day. Accidents did happen, and as well we had a thousand on the staff. If we could enlist some staff to undertake a first-aid course, perhaps we could look after those two days ourselves.

The first Saturday this master plan was put into operation, a pregnant lady's waters broke in the elevator. Sister was back.

An urgent call came, announcing a gunman was outside menswear. A known bank-robber had been seen by a bank manager on the ground floor. It was 9.45am and the bank was in no danger, but the bank manager was. He pursued the man up three flights of stairs. The gunman turned around and shot him in the chest.

I watched the colour drain from the manager's body, and could not help thinking that he gave away his life for nothing. Common sense kicked in and I became scared. Where was the gunman? Have the police been called?

They had been called and caught up with the man in Avoca NSW, a few weeks later. The gunman was killed in a shoot-out.

We had good profits and a few losses. One of our department mangers saw a man struggling with a large TV set as he made his way out to the car park. The manager said, "Here - let me help," and helped him to his car. The 'customer' had stolen the set.

One day what started out to be routine piece of mischief turned into a first class crisis. One of our storemen had again acted offensively. I had given him three warnings as required by the politically correct award and it was in the best interests of the store that he did not come in again. Before you knew it, the delivery trucks lined up in the street and refused to enter our loading dock. The union secretary appeared as if by magic and ordered the offender to be re-instated.

Grace Bros. would not support my action if it meant closing the store, especially as this was December. When dealing with unions you must have at least a two-pronged approach. You know they are going to beat you on one argument, for after all they have to prove to the worker that they have muscle and will use it on their behalf. But if you have two items, they will let you win one. I had two. First, he had to be sacked, Second, he had been employed for 7 years. At that time it was not compulsory to pay out pro rata long service leave. My decision was that he lose his job and be given no pro rata long service money. The argument played out and the trucks were still in the street.

A caller from head office almost screamed down the phone, "I hope you know what you are doing!" For a while it looked as though I was the one to lose his job. Finally I conceded that if the union agreed the dismissal was proper, I may consider making the money available. This is what I had planned all along anyway. The union boss finally agreed to the compromise and took the employee aside telling him, "You deserved all you got mate, but the union stood by you and we have demanded you get your pro rata long service money."

The trucks began to roll and the stock was being unloaded at a fast rate of knots. As the unionist departed I could not help thinking of my defeat over the opening day strike. I had since stopped attending Sydney University. There was no point learning industrial law. Unions don't act according to law. They put forward claims knowing that are asking too much, but they want to see how much they can win. The employers, on the other hand, must go into bat to find out how little they can lose. It's all a matter of who has the best negotiating skills.

Feeling very satisfied, I reminded myself of my vow of twelve months ago: "When the next stoush comes, I going to win."

For Valour

Bob and Dolly Dyer walked into a little wooden Presbyterian Church and sat in front of me. The first thing that came to mind was that I was not going to see a great deal. He was a mountain of a man. Television in the 1960s belonged to Bob Dyer (Howdy customers!).

His great show was Pick-a-Box, where he gave the option to the contestants of choosing a box, which could contain financial rewards or a safety pin. The audience went wild, some advising to choose the box, others saying keep the prize already earned, and take no chances. The show rated its head off.

One of the most memorable contestants was a slow-talking banana grower from the small farming community of Macksville, approx. 300 miles north of Sydney on the Pacific Highway. He seemed to possess a photographic memory and his simple approach endeared him to the audience as he increased his take in the prize pool.

In 1856, just after the Crimean War, Queen Victoria instituted a new award for gallantry in the field. It should be highly prized and sought after. Of all the medals and decorations, the Victoria Cross is the highest ranking. The Victoria Cross (VC), consists of a Maltese Cross with the Royal Crest in the centre and bares the words 'For Valour.' The medal is cast in bronze and oddly enough the metal comes from one of the Russian guns which was captured in Sebastopol. The gentle, intelligent brave banana grower who won the hearts of the television audience won the Victoria Cross as a soldier in the Australian Army during World War 11.

For many years Frank and his father Paddy made their living growing bananas. In the early sixties Frank married a Sydney nursing sister and began to build the marital home. His main form of transport was an old Hillman Ute, which would chug along at a top speed of 30 mph. Deciding to upgrade, Frank became the proud owner of a Volkswagen. His tragic death occurred on a country road. He went under a timber jinker.

There was no way the Military brass and mourners were going to cram into a small church but the crowd said their good-byes as they walked behind the gun carriage which bore his coffin. It was my privilege to meet Frank on various occasions. His replies were well weighted and not quick to come but when you spoke to Frank Partridge you knew you were speaking to a great man.

In 1994 I was a guest of a member of the Union Jack Club in London. A feature of the Club was the varnished walls, which bore the names of all the Victoria Cross winners. I moved along the walls and stopped at the name of Partridge. He made Macksville proud.

Whilst the Victoria Cross award was instituted in 1856, it was made retrospective to 1845 in order to incorporate the period of the Crimean War. In 1854 the British Fleet was in the Baltic. It was 21 June when the fleet closed in to attack the fortress of Bomarsund at short range. The fortress did not give in easily and trained its eighty guns on the invaders.

It was during this attack that a live shell fell on the deck of the HMS Hecla. Without hesitation the mate leaped forward, picked up the shell and hurled it into the sea. It exploded as it hit the water. This courageous action saved the lives of many and he was immediately promoted to Lieutenant.

Three years later this gallant Lieutenant, Charles Lucas was presented with the first Victoria Cross. He went on to become a Rear Admiral. Lucas died in August 1914.

Bob Dyer was confronted with another famous contestant when he found Barry Jones in the chair. Barry Jones was not a Victoria Cross winner but one of the most highly intelligent politicians in the Australian Parliament. He was Minister for Science in the Hawke Government and the national president of the ALP in 1992.

On rare occasions the official answers supplied were not quite correct. Barry Jones had no hesitation in putting the matter right. It was hilarious to see Bob Dyer give up and shake his head as Barry sorted out the problems.

Ronald Ryan was hanged in Melbourne's Pentridge Jail on 3 February 1967. The city seemed to come to a halt as trams and cars pulled to a halt and church bells pealed out their disapproval. Ryan's execution was the last in Australia. Barry Jones took up the fight to prevent the hanging. Further, he wanted the death penalty abolished. Barry Jones commented that the execution of Ronald Ryan left a scar in his mind that would never heal.

After failing to prevent the hanging, Barry Jones was traumatised, taking some weeks to recover. He shared his sorrow by saying that after the execution of Ryan he went home and lay on his bed all day, staring at the ceiling. In a thoughtful speech he made a statement that burned into the hearts of all who heard and read it. Henry Bolte was the Victorian premier and he supported the hanging. The high point of Jones's speech must surely be, "I doubt if Ryan had an intention to kill, but I am certain that Bolte did."

The American counterpart of the Victoria Cross is the Medal of Honour - the highest award for valour in the American Defence Force. One of the most decorated American soldiers in WWII was the son of very poor Texas sharecroppers. His name was Audie Murphy. Young Audie lied about his age and attempted to join the army after the bombing of Pearl Harbour.

He was a mere fifteen years old. Audie's sister got to work on the certificate and made him eighteen. Audie was of slight build and under five feet, six inches in height. The Marines and Paratroopers both turned him down. He also had the problem of having a 'baby-face' appearance.

Finally, the Army took him in and fought the system that tried to give him a non-combat role. Audie soon proved he was a soldier and became a legend in the 3rd Infantry Division. Fighting in the front line he was credited with killing 240 of the enemy, wounding and capturing many others. He rose to the rank of staff sergeant and then to 2nd Lieutenant. Audie was wounded three times, but fought in nine major campaigns across Europe.

After the war he became a successful actor, appearing in 44 American films. It is said his best movie was 'Red Badge of Courage', (hardly surprising) and 'To Hell and Back'. Both movies were based on his war experiences. His Medal of Honour topped off a list a many decorations which included, DSC, Silver Star, Legion of Merit Purple heart with Oak Clusters, to name a few. He was killed in a plane crash in Virginia.

When actions like those are considered it raises two questions in my mind. The first is, why was incompetent leadership allowed to command for such a long period of time? Of all the perpetrators of stupidity the prize must be awarded to General Sir Douglas H, commander of the British Expeditionary Force in WW 1. The Germans had taken Belgium and Northern France and it was up to the Allies to remove them. The French were forced to hand over command to General Haig.

Records reveal that the command was one of mass slaughter. At the Battle of the Somme, July 1, 1916 – November 9, 1916, it was recorded that over one million were dead and this number included 420,000 British troops. It was Frank Murdoch, father of Rupert Murdoch who faced the British Government with the challenge of bad leadership that cost so many Australian lives during WW I.

The ordinary soldier could see the dangers of inept leadership. A machine-gunner at the battle of the Somme described what he saw when the troops were expected to get through German reinforcing wire. He asked; "How did our planners imagine we could get through the wire? Who told them that artillery fire would pound the wire to pieces? Any Tommy could have told them that shellfire lifts wire up and drops it down often in a worse tangle than before." An anonymous soldiers' song was born that day, it was named 'Over The Top'.

Lowell Tarling

Lowell lives in the Blue Mountains, NSW. He paints, teaches and writes for a living. Check out his paintings at True Bean Café, Katoomba Street. Lowell keeps a diary, writes song-poems and occasional novels, interviewing interesting people and writing the biography of Tiny Tim.
www.lowelltarling.com.au

To Catch a Thief

It is 5 November. Today the real estate agent tells us that if all goes to plan with the sale of the house, we will need to be out by 27 November. We're moving into Mick and Jeannine Reid's 3-bedroom flat in Katoomba central. This means putting 3000 books in Kennards Storage. I have to reduce.

And then the phone rings. It's my father who wants to know what time I'll be at the bookshop where I work, because he feels uneasy about someone he met last Thursday and wants to talk about it. It is a stranger who contacted him about Bible Studies out of the blue, then attempted to discuss his bank accounts. I tell my father I'll be at the shop at 10.30.

It's going to rain today, it's one of those days where the till expects to be disappointed. However, I make a respectable total between 10.30-2.30 behind the counter, after which nothing at all happens. No Luke, no Dave McMahon, no Lisa, not the guy who calls me Bro, nobody… and yes – it rains. Chris has broken a shelf, all the Sport books are on the counter with a note saying, 'Would you…?' I've got nothing else to do, I didn't bring my laptop so - sure Chris, I'll tidy. But I want to read a couple of chapters about Brett Whiteley first.

My father phones to check I'm at the shop and says he'll be there soon. He rides up on his old-person's scooter, walks in pensively, sits on the high chair and tells me about this stranger. His name is Allan John Quinn, my father hands me a slip of paper in his own handwriting, which has his address and phone number.

After phoning my father for Bible studies, my father agreed to see him. So Quinn called last Thursday and told him that he had spent seven years in jail. He showed my father a wad of press clippings. While in prison he didn't have much to read except a Bible and finished up more impressed than he expected. In fact, he has decided to live for Christ and thinks my father should give him Bible studies. (That's odd, I note – my father is a former schoolteacher, not a Minister of Religion.)

And so they chatted last Thursday in my father's retirement village flat until Quinn suggested they go someplace for a coffee. Off they went to Northgate and chatted about the Bible some more. On the way back, there was a very different conversation.

Quinn said there was just one thing he really felt he ought to put right – before the Lord – as it were. He owed $19,000 to a woman, which was a terrible burden to his conscience. My father ignored the bait. It pained Quinn to have such a thing between him and Jesus, and if only he could clear the matter up, then everything would be straight. My father didn't respond.

As they drove down William Street, Quinn poured out his predicament. When they pulled up outside the Seventh-day Adventist Retirement Village, Quinn dropped the money subject and talked instead about friendship, 'We're friends now,' he insisted, 'friends!' My father said, 'yes.' I mean, why not? My Dad hasn't got a lot to do all day.

Allan John Quinn is who my father is telling me about in the Bookshop as I sell three Feists to a customer. I am thinking of shelf space around F in Science Fiction. Raymond Feist books are never skinny, I reckon that gives us another four inches.

'I think I'll phone him up,' I reply, seeking the slip of paper with the phone number beside the calculator on the desk.

'Would you? That would relieve me of a burden,' my father replies, as if I am doing him a big favour. (*It's only a phone call, mate.*) 'I can't understand how he got my name?' Throughout this saga, this question is never answered.

Two hours later, while I'm tidying Sport, my father phones.

'Have you called him yet?'

'I've tried twice, no response. I'll see you after work.'

I call around 5.30 and report I've tried the number six times, no answer – it went to an answering machine.

'Did you leave your details on it?'

'No, he doesn't know that I exist.'

'Good.'

I confirm that I'll be present next time my father sees Quinn, which is Thursday 1.00. I suggest that I vanish into the toilet as soon as he knocks and not come out until the conversation has settled down – maybe on the subject of money. This will surprise Quinn, he'll say something like, 'I didn't know anyone else was here.' Then I'll say 'What were we all talking about?' and join the conversation with a view to questioning him as to why he is so interested in my father's assets. *Secret Detective Lowell on the job, suh!*

Next morning I search the Net, and look what comes up!

15 April 2005 - Helpful Conman Has Jail Term Cut: A confessed conman who preyed on the elderly in three states will walk from prison next week as a reward for helping catch a Queensland serial killer. Allan John Quinn, 53, pretended to be a bank official so he could steal money from the accounts of the victims. In a case quoted by an appeal court judge yesterday, Quinn swapped a passbook he was carrying with one owned by a 92-year old man. Over two days Quinn withdrew more than $18,000 from the man's account before a suspicious bank teller stopped an attempt to take another $4400. Quinn obtained more than $60,000 in Victoria, $300,000 in NSW, plus $100,000 from various fraudulent schemes…the decision means Quinn is eligible to leave prison within the next week, but will potentially have 14 months to serve if he reoffends'.

Robbie wants me to contact the Police immediately; I want to think about it first. Think, think, think, yep - she's right. So I drive to Hornsby Police and ask to speak to someone 'about a crime which is about to be committed'. The lady cop behind the counter looks startled, glances at my red shoulder bag and asks what this is about? I tell her in a sentence. She tells me to take a seat.

I sit beside a mother and daughter and read the Sandra McGrath *Brett Whiteley* paperback. Who knows how long this is going to take? After 45 minutes they are taken into a side room by a uniformed Police Officer, and from the little I overhear it sounds like a domestic dispute.

Suddenly the door bursts open and this big smiley guy, Det Snr Constable Steve Hungerford invites me to come on through. He walks me past a hallway with Award Certificates on the wall, a water dispenser and lots of doors. *Men's* – that's the door I'm looking for right now, after drinking that Red Bull.

He invites me into a small interrogation room where I explain that although nothing has happened, a crime is about to be committed. I expect him to reply, 'If no crime has been committed, I've got better things to do with my time.' But no, he says he'll be the judge of that and he studies the Internet entry I pass him, hears me out. I get the feeling he loathes people like Quinn. He mutters phrases like, 'preying on old people' and 'let's put this guy behind bars *where he belongs.*' I can't thank him enough.

I do my best but there are certain questions I can't properly answer, so I tell him I could go fetch my father who lives only five minutes away. 'Absolutely,' says the detective, 'I want to talk to him.'

I phone my father – 'The Police?' he says in a quavering voice.

'Yes Dad, the Police, and I'm coming round to get you now.'

Well, he's not too sure about the Police. He insists no crime has been committed. Nevertheless he agrees for me to fetch him. Now there are two of us in the room with Det Snr Constable Hungerford. I try to say as little as possible, because I don't want to feed my father lines.

The detective asks my father whether Quinn opened any drawers or looked around his flat. My father says no. I interject that the flat is so small that if Quinn went to the toilet he'd be walking through the bedroom where some valuable are kept. 'No,' my father replies, 'He didn't go to the toilet.'

'Did you go to the kitchen and get him something to drink?' says the detective. 'No,' replies my father, 'we went to Westfield's for a drink.'

'What was the name of the café?'

'I can't recall.'

'This guy, what did he look like?'

'Well he was big…' says my father.

'Hair colour?'

'Don't know.'

'Age?'

'Maybe my son's age…'

'Which is?'

'Mid-50s.'

'What kind of car did he drive?'

'Don't know – maybe something late model Japanese.'

'What colour was it?'

'Don't know.'

The Det Snr Constable picks up a road map, checks out the Schofield address and notes it doesn't appear to be a built-up area. 'The address is fake, you can count on it', he slaps the book shut, pauses for thought, flicks through his notes then looks at us candidly and says, 'I think we'll pick this bloke up. When did you say he was coming around?'

'1.00 Thursday,' my father replies. 'But I really must stress, no crime has been committed.'

Det Snr Constable Hungerford is unmoved, 'We'll get a couple of plain clothes officers around there around 12.30.'

Now I get jumpy, it's my turn, 'What do I do? What will happen then? Will he come to the door? Do you want me to hide in the toilet??'

I don't think that he much cares what I do. 'And how do I work the Bookplate into the story? because I've been writing stories about the shop and nothing much happens. We need a thief. I must have said that aloud, 'The Bookplate,' I explain – 'I work there on Sundays.'

'The secondhand bookshop! I go there sometimes!' I now want to know what the Det Snr Constable reads – Sci-Fi, I bet.

So I drop my father outside his place and drive home. The mobile rings, I pull over, ear to phone. My father says Quinn was at his door when he arrived home 10 minutes ago but my father dismissed him saying 'Thursday was the agreed day.' I phone Det Snr Constable Hungerford to tell him this. He seems appreciative of the call, also surprised.

Three hours later my father is back on the line saying Quinn just phoned wanting to know if everything is all right, are they still friends? My father told him yes but explained to Quinn that when he got home he needed a sleep and can't remember anything about the house call. Quinn then asked about my father's situation with credit cards, to which my father said he didn't use them. Bank accounts? My father explained that he was not rich, 'But what about the units,' said Quinn, 'You've got three of those.'

'How did he know about the units?' I burst.

'I probably told him,' my father admits. 'But what I can't understand is how did he know to contact me?'

'That's what we aim to find out, Dad, on Thursday.'

My cunning plan hasn't changed much since I first thought of it. It is to arrive at 12.30, when Quinn knocks I hide in the toilet, come out when the conversation has settled down, then say 'Oh you're my father's new friend - let me snap your photograph' – do it early, because the more he gets to know me, the easier it becomes to say no to a snap. And the Police? Well, I'm not sure - they'll probably arrest him when he leaves the premises. That's the plan, I reckon.

Three days later, on Thursday – around 10.00 - I phone Hornsby Police and am assigned to Det Snr Constable Sally Johnston who knows the case and will be at my father's place at 12.30. 'I'll be there too!' I reply.

Then Det Snr Constable Steve Hungerford phones to tell me he has other business to attend to this morning and that Det Snr Constable Sally Johnston will take care of the matter. I tell him I just spoke with Sally five minutes ago, so that's all right. But he clearly he can't stand people who rip off oldies. 'What a bastard!' he says. I reckon who wants to cheat on oldies should give this cop a real wide berth.

Thursday: around 11.30 drive to St Ives to buy two pens. While I'm there, the phone rings. My father says, 'He's coming earlier than expected, he's on his way now.'

'How long do you reckon before he arrives?'

'10-15 minutes.'

I dial Hornsby Police and get through to Sally. 'We'll be there immediately!' And they are.

Meanwhile I take longer than normal to drive to Hornsby, there is a traffic incident at the major intersection near the bridge, so I have plenty of time to think about what to do when I get to the house.

Hiding in the toilet – is a must for every amateur detective. Next, how to confront Quinn? Maybe I'll have to do a Citizen's Arrest – which I don't know anything about. And what if he tries to run off? I know – I'll close the glass doors to the whole complex to delay his escape for long enough for the Police to grab him. But how can I close those outside doors if I'm hiding in the inside toilet? A plan, a plan, a cunning plan – what is it?

The Policeman waves me through the traffic, I drive to William Street and arrive at the house. I park behind a 4-wheel drive maroon Mitsubishi, I write the number plate Y66 272 in my diary – well...it might be a 'clue'.

As I walk up the steps I see one of the elderly women standing on the upper verandah watching the door of my father's unit. *Knock knock* - my father opens up to a roomful of four people. The manager of the flats –is in the room laughing uproariously and proclaiming in a big voice, 'Wow, the Police!'

Sally – *we meet at last* – she shakes my hand, and introduces me to Det Snr Constable Steve Houston who is a very solidly built severe looking guy. I'd be scared of him, if he didn't like me. Meanwhile Kevin is generating heaps of sound, 'I didn't think we'd have the Police here!'

'Do you think you could say The Police any louder Kevin?' I tug his arm. 'Let's go, go' and he leaves with me, he's chuckling of course. Walking towards the front of the building Kevin loudly proclaims, 'They weren't even in uniform!' He goes upstairs to his unit, no doubt peering over the verandah because of what is about to happen next.

I wait at the front of the building, checking out the glass door that I might have to dramatically close if Quinn does a runner. I'm writing down all number plates and hanging around the front trying not to look conspicuous.

Here comes a car, could this be Quinn? Nope, it drives straight past. Another car - *Detective Lowell* on the case, looking casual – whistling in fact – could this be the car? Nope, it whizzes past. After about 10 of these it occurs to me that I am one possibly one of the least conspicuous people in Hornsby. I am carrying a bright red shoulder bag depicting a colourful picture of a bleeding heart Jesus. I wear red/blue glasses, plus I am walking up and down the front of the retirement village, whistling. Most people don't do that.

Another car – too new – blasts past.

Secret Detective Lowell will hide in the foliage, as in the movies. This is most uncomfortable. I walk across to the car park, sit on a stack of bricks, put my bag out of sight and write in my diary whatever happens next, which is, *A gold- coloured car drives past cautiously – it looks that this might be the car, but it drives past like all the others. After a few minutes it drives back, pulls up behind mine. And a guy in a singlet gets out...*' I stop writing.

He takes ages before getting out. Eventually he opens backdoor, organises something and closes that door. Then, he walks up the steps, pushes open the glass door of the retirement village and heads towards my father's unit. I follow. When certain he is inside I enter the room and find that Quinn has already been introduced to Detectives Sally Johnston and Steve Houston. They're straight in:

Det Snr Constable Steven Houston: *How did you know to contact Rowland Tarling?*

Quinn: Oh, through some guys I know.

Who are they?

Quinn: They go to church over Wahroonga somewhere.

Which church is that?

Quinn: The Seventh-day Adventist one.

Dad: *This is my son, Lowell.*

(shakes hands) Allan Quinn.

Lowell: *Hello Allan*

Quinn: (to the Police) And his son, he is an author, so I wanted to show him my book.

Houston: *What's your background Allan?*

Quinn: Why? What's the problem?

Houston: *Well we're a bit concerned with you just turning up out of the blue here.*

Quinn: I phoned him, I said, I said, I said, do you want me to come and talk to you? Last time I saw him I said, 'Do you want to see me and talk to me?' and he said yeah, so there's no problem.

Houston: *Have you got some ID on you mate?*

Quinn: Yeah. I've done nothing wrong, I don't have to talk to you.

Houston: *Well, we think different.*

Johnston: *We need to check who you are first Allan, see - we deal with people like you all the time.*

Quinn: What do you mean 'people like me'?

Well we've read your rough sheet. You do this quite a bit, don't you?

Quinn: Yeah, but what do you mean?

Johnston: *Come and speak to elderly people in nursing homes and* churches and places like that?

Quinn: Yes, but I've done nothing here.

Houston: *Is that the address you gave this fella?* (pointing at my Dad). *You've got my name and address, telephone number, everything.*

Lowell: *Your address is not in a built-up area on the map though? What's that? If you look on a map - where you live is in a green area, it doesn't look like a housing area? Do you live in an industrial zone?*

Quinn: No, residential. I just wanted to get some information about you for a book I'm doing.

Lowell: *How did you come across my father's name?*

Quinn: Someone told me he's got a son who's a successful author and that sort of thing…

Lowell: *What guy were you talking to?*

Quinn: Some guys over coffee.

Lowell: *What sort of guys were these? What's their names?*

Quinn::I can't remember names. I just wanted to get some tips for my book, that's why I brought the book here today.

And he holds up his book. It's called *Predator*.

What's that then? Says Det Houston pointing to the book and CD-Rom.

Quinn holds in his hand.

Quinn: A book I wrote.

Johnston: *Really?*

Quinn: Yeah, I'm an author.

Johnston: *You can understand the concerns we have about you, can't you? Coming to see old people and then you start questioning about Visa accounts.*

Quinn: I didn't do that.

Johnston: *You didn't do that over the phone?*

Quinn: No.

Johnston: *No?*

Quinn: Not at all.

Lowell: *Yes you did. You asked my father about his credit cards and bank accounts.*

Quinn: No I didn't.

Lowell: *Then how do I know that detail?*

Quinn: A hundred per cent I didn't ask him about Visa accounts, credit cards or anything.

Houston: *(looming above Quinn) All right – we're placing you under arrest for intent to repeat an indictable offence, do you understand that? Anything you say or do may later be used as evidence, do you understand that Allan?*

Quinn: But I've done nothing wrong, sir.

Johnston: *For intent to repeat an indictable offence you've been charged...*

Houston: *You've been seeing this old fella over here with the intent to commit another fraud offence, that's what we're alleging, okay?*

Quinn: But I ain't done nothing wrong.

Johnston: *You have a talk to the Courts about that, okay?*

(raised voices)

Johnston: *You're also circulated on our system for being suspect for other matters mate.*

Quinn: What matters?

Houston *We'll explain it back at the Police Station. Have you got your car keys there, we'll have a look through your car as well.*

Det Steve Houston takes him out, Sally Johnston turns to us and says, 'We're going to take him back to the Police Station now, I'll give you a ring on your mobile when we get there and have a chat to you then.'

'*Come on Allan,*' says Steve, nodding at me and saying, 'We'll give you a call.'

Sally Johnston takes down my statement. She tells me Quinn has appeared on the *Australia's Most Wanted* TV show, then she talks about attending a wedding in Bermagui (where we used to live).

Once he'd got his man, Steve Houston was totally genial. Plus I saw Steve Hungerford again, he came in from another job just as we were leaving and asked how things panned out. As for my father, I said goodbye to him in a room where Det Snr Constable Houston was trying to take his Statement. Sally warned me they were going to take ages, and if I needed to get away, they would drive my father home.

I ask Steve Houston whether my father told him that he was an Interrogator in World War 2. 'Yes, he has actually.' 'And about his high school, St Walter St John's?' 'Er-yes.' 'Has he sung any Gilbert & Sullivan?' Steve starts to laugh.

As for Quinn, right up to the last my father was worried that he had done an injustice to someone who might have genuinely wanted to turn to Jesus. 'What if he really *did* want Bible studies?' said my father who phoned me later in the afternoon.

The outcome is this—Quinn will be released, if he contacts my father, he will be imprisoned.

Back home, my wife Robbie says, 'Last week you were complaining there wasn't any action in your bookshop stories!'

'This isn't a story about the bookshop.'

'It is,' she replies, 'if you tie it in at the end.'

'What? By saying: *I passed the Bookplate and thought I should call in and tell this story to Chris, because he's there on Thursdays…*'

'Yes,' says Robbie, 'That'll do.'

Jam Studio, Gosford

'I think we're losing him,' says Genna, peering at Robert through the studio glass.

'Yesterday I said to him, *you don't need me...*' I reply.

'Really?'

'I said, *You write better words than me.*'

'What did he say?'

'He said he'll always need me because he writes heaps more tunes than words.'

We're sitting here with Paul Bryant recording *Have Your Heard The News*. Sally is somewhere else, crying.

Robert is on the studio floor listening to arranger Charlie Hull talking to musos Mick Reid, Graham Jesse, John Coker, Ron Papos in an incomprehensible manner. 'It's a ch-pow-bicka/bicka/bicka.'

'No,' someone says, 'It's ch-pow/*pow*-bicka/bicka/bicka.'

'Sorry, you're quite right,' says Charlie, 'Ch-pow/*pow*-bicka/bicka/bicka, but a nice and long chhh.'

'They're not doing it right,' I tell Genna, 'All they need is a good hard G-C strum, that's what Sally's used to and it's what Mick should be doing on that 12-string guitar.'

'Just a tip for you Lowell,' says Paul, glancing at Genna, 'Do yourself a favour and don't bother telling Mick Reid how to play guitar.'

'But they've upset Sally,' I press, 'She doesn't sing it like that, I know how she sings it. It doesn't have that bass stuff, it's just straight – **ONE** – 2 – 3 – 4, **ONE** – 2 – 3 – 4…like that.'

'Don't worry about it Lowell,' Genna sighs, putting his arm around my shoulders.

'But they've made Sally cry!'

The studio door opens and out comes Robert and Charlie, laughing about something. Ch-pow/*pow*-bicka/bicka/bicka. Mick – who dresses like an urban cowboy, in jeans and heeled boots, puts his 12-string guitar down, picks up his Telecaster and Robert says, 'Where's Sally? I think we've got it, and I want her to hear it. Is everything all right?'

'Guess so.'

Then Robert and Charlie talk about the affects they want to try on Sally's voice, an Aural Exciter – 'like Linda Ronstadt' - says Robert.

'Like dribbling on your chin,' says Charlie.

Sam walks in the door carrying his guitar, gives Genna a handshake, Paul a nod, Robert a hug and says, 'What's happened to you?' as he sees my walking stick and the awkwardness with which I stand.

'I've only been out of hospital four weeks,' I reply. 'It's a minor leg injury.'

'How's Robbie and the kids?'

'Fine.'

'But you're not,' Sam laughs, slapping my arm and moving on. 'This is Charlie and Mick…' says Robert, and back they all go into the studio, this time with Sam. The song is *Bringing To You*.

'That's a blast from the past,' Robert laughs.

Then Genna comes back, the boys are back in the studio, and I ask. 'Is she all right?'

'She is now.'

'What did you tell her?'

'I said we are in a position to define Gospel Music in Australia.'

'That's what you said?' I reply.

'Yep.'

'And she said?'

'She said, *Who is we, white man?*'

'Bloody teenager!'

'Well,' Genna concludes, 'She was upset until I made her laugh. Now she's going to give it another shot.'

'Well she's now got Sam and he's backed her before – with me - maybe he'll know how to handle her.'

'How are you getting on with the musos?' questions Genna.

'Fine,' I reply, 'so long as I don't speak.'

'Robert and Mick swapped phone numbers…'

'Plus I overheard them talking about Ricky Skaggs and John Prine, so they're on the same wavelength, I guess.'

'Who's Ricky Skaggs?' says Genna.

Sally sits with Genna, Paul and me, while Charlie, Mick, Sam and John Coker lay something down.

'You know what I reckon Genna,' I begin.

'No!' says Paul, raising a finger, 'Don't express an opinion. They don't need any distractions. Sally? Are you getting the hang of the song?'

'I think so,' she replies.

This time she's perfect and all the boys make a big fuss, telling her how great she is and would she like to join us at the Gosford Chinese joint for nosh-up?

According to Paul, I'm not supposed to come in with suggestions that sound like the Bonzo Dog Band. 'It won't help.' So we talk about Punk Rock. Robert won't admit the Sex Pistols as a proper band because 'they can't play'. He likes J J Cale, Ry Cooder and Linda Ronstadt. He also likes Bob James. Leaving the Sex Pistols aside, Robert agrees Randy Newman, Bob Dylan, Ian Dury and especially Dire Straits are great bands.

'You know what Mick Reid said about Dire Straits?' Robert says, over Beef & Black Bean Sauce, Chicken Chow Mein and a curry dish that looks yellow and sweaty. I avoid the curry.

'What did he say?'

'He said when Mark Knofler recorded *Sultans of Swing* it sent all the guitarists back to the drawing board.'

Back to the Sex Pistols. Robert insists you simply can't be a musician if you can't play your instrument.

We wrangle about Punk Rock while munching fried rice and garlic prawns, finally drawing a truce when Robert declares that I am a 'phenomenologist' because 'the phenomenon's the thing'. I'm happy with that.

'I know Lowell, that you'd rather have something that sounds like the Saints, but…' Robert draws our attention to Gospel acts like Michael O'Martian, André Crouch and Keith Green. He suggests Genna and Sally should pay attention to these musicians too. That's kinda what we're doing.

But the phenomenologist tag amuses Genna heaps. 'Phenomenologist!' he chuckles, when there's nothing else to say. He loves the word.

Then – mid-meal - Mick Reid walks in and says Charlie can't be here because he had to go home. He pulls up a chair next to Robert and orders food. Mick is keen about an idea of turning *Carried Away* into a calypso, and Robert is enchanted by the idea. We lose Robert on all that talk. Genna bickers with Paul about I don't know what. So Sally and I talk about school. And the Beatles.

'The point is Sally,' I find myself saying, 'The Beatles did everything. They were avant garde take – *Revolution No 9*!'

This gets Mick's attention. Surprise, surprise! He agrees with me about the Beatles but for different reasons. 'Never mind *Revolution No 9*,' he laughs dismissively, 'there's *Michelle, Hold Me Tight*, and great lyrics like, *She was just seventeen, you know what I mean*, How tight is that?'

'But were they a product of their time or did they create it?' questions Genna, as if we weren't already argumentative enough.

The issue is: *the inevitably of genius* - with Mick on his second beer. Mick believes in the inevitability of genius, I don't. Genna sides with me and Robert probably agrees with us, even though he's helping Mick's case.

'I think we're losing him,' says Genna about Robert, when he can't hear.

And then I snap at the waiter, for putting onion – 'poison' I call it – in my food. I bang my walking stick on the floor and tell this delicate Chinese waiter that I specifically said 'no onion'.

Sally is taken aback – she's seen me calm as a lake, dealing with a restless Fourth Form (Year 10). Now this. Robert knows it's got nothing to do with the inevitably of genius. Sam is startled. Mick probably thinks I'm a rude bugger. And after checking whether Paul Bryant has upset me and I say no, Genna can't understand me either.

But there's onion in my food and this hollow pain in my right leg.

'How long since you've had a general anaesthetic?' asks Genna.

'Four weeks.'

'Well,' Genna replies, reverting to his role as a medico, 'The after-effects of a general actually remains in your system at least eight weeks'.

Having embarrassed myself, we pay the bill and leave.

'I'm going to limp for the rest of my life Genna!' I exclaim, as we walk along the street. 'I'm a bloody cripple. I've been in hospital forever, poor Roy Wilkinson is still in there, so is Jane! All my friends are cripples!'

'All *my* friends are sinners,' laughs Genna, as we cross Mann Street.

I stop in the middle of the traffic, knowing drivers wouldn't dare hit a guy with a cane.

'That's the title of the album – *All My Friends Are Sinners*!' I exclaim. 'You said it!'

Robert and Sally say, yeah!

Murray McLeod

Murray McLeod is an established author and illustrator with his motorcycle, aviation books and magazines. Murray's meticulous writing style is matched by his attention to detail in his artwork.
See www.mcleodart.com.au

Lt. Frank McNamara VC, Flying ace

Frank McNamara is included in the British aces as the sole Australian in the exalted company of the 19 air V.C.s of World War 1. Australia's initial involvement in military aviation began in August 1914 with the creation of a flying school at Point Cook in Victoria. At the time of the Gallipoli campaign Britain made a request for Australia to provide personnel for overseas service.

The force was known as the First Half Flight, and after a brief spell in India it proceeded to Mesopotamia where it began operations against Turkish forces in that area.

In a brief and hazardous campaign they carried out photographic missions deep into enemy territory. Two airmen were forced down and presumed murdered by hostile Bedouin and nine others became prisoners of war. In September 1916 four squadrons including the Half Flight were raised to form the Australian Flying Corps. No.1 remained in the Middle East while 2, 3 and 4 moved to France and the Western Front.

McNamara joined No.1 Squadron at that period and began operations on the BE2, which formed their original equipment. The BE2 proved to be quite inadequate on the Western Front. But in the less hazardous Middle East theatre it performed reasonably well, although engine failure was a frequent occurrence in that harsh environment.

That situation faced Captain D. Rutherford in June 1917 when his Be2 was forced down near a party of Turkish troops. Lt. McNamara, piloting a single-seat Martynside G102 observed Rutherford's plight and made a rescue attempt. He suffered severe wounding from ground fire as he landed beside the disabled Be2.

With Rutherford clinging to a wing strut he attempted a take-off from the uneven surface. Weakened by his wound he lost control and in the ensuing crash his machine was wrecked.

They scrambled from the wrecked Martynside, set it alight, then transferred to Rutherford's Be2. McNamara took over the controls while Rutherford swung the prop. In a stroke of good fortune the engine started. The intrepid pair made a second getaway attempt. Pursued by mounted troops they gathered speed and made a dramatic escape with Rutherford again clinging to a wing strut.

Despite the agony of his wound and loss of blood McNamara remained conscious long enough to make a safe return to base, some 60 miles away. McNamara recovered from his wound and for his determination and courage he was awarded the Victoria Cross. Captain Rutherford suffered a later misfortune when he experienced another forced landing. In a rescue attempt that was almost a repeat of the McNamara incident a brother officer crashed his own machine. But on that occasion there was no dramatic rescue and both pilots became prisoners of war.

(An excerpt from 'Images of Eagles')

Ken Rosewall

Few, in any top-rank players can match the longevity of Ken Rosewall's remarkable tennis career. Taking Wimbledon as an example, Rosewall first reached the singles final in 1953 against J. Drobny at age 18 , followed by appearances in 1956 (Lewis Hoad) and 1970 (John Newcombe), until his Wimbledon swan-song in 1974 (Jimmy Connors); an incredible twenty one year span at the quintessential tennis tournament!

Unfortunately for Rosewall, in all these finals appearances that prestigious Wimbledon title was to be denied him. However in the Australian championship he claimed the title in 1953 and again in 1972 to create the biggest gap between first and last singles titles at that tournament.

Kenneth Robert Rosewall was born 2 November 1934 in Sydney, Australia into a family with an involvement in tennis. The youngster was a natural left-hander, however his father coached him to play right-handed; the outcome of this unorthodoxy was the development of an effective backhand, which has been generally considered as the best yet seen. An adverse result was a relatively weak forehand and serve, nevertheless he was fast, agile and tireless, and with a punishing volley.

Rosewall's early career paralleled that of Sydneysider Lewis Hoad, slightly younger than Rosewall, they became great rivals in singles, and paired in doubles, a champion combination. Rosewall was possibly the better junior, although Hoad surpassed him later, as an amateur and also in his early professional days. Hoad's stellar career was sadly terminated by an ongoing back injury, even allowing for that it was unlikely that Hoad could have sustained the standard of play that Rosewall delivered year by year.

Not surprisingly in their junior days Rosewall and Hoad were labelled the 'tennis twins'; a period when they won the Australian Junior singles and doubles titles three years in a row (1950, 1951 and 1952) Their arrival in senior tennis was a timely one for Australia'a Davis Cup aspirations, following Cup stalwarts Sedgman and McGregor's move to the professional scene. Hoad had been a non-playing member of the 1952 squad, and in 1953 the 'twins' became the lead players for that year's cup defence; other team members were Rex Hartwig and Mervyn Rose.

Earlier that year Roswall had won the Australian and French singles, and with Hoad, both doubles. Later in the same year Hoad won the NSW, Victorian and Queensland singles and with Rosewall the NSW doubles. Hopes were high that might even hold the Cup. The Cup venue was Melbourne's Kooyong tennis complex, with the US team spearheaded by Vic Seixas and Tony Trabert. In previous encounters Hoad had been beaten twice by Seixas, and in America Rosewall had suffered defeat by Trabert; raising the question; would the 'twins' be strong enough?

Hoad answered one part of the question by defeating Seixas convincingly in the opening singles rubber; unfortunately Rosewall was overpowered by Trabert; leaving the series at one-all. Perhaps the selectors showed a lack of faith in Rosewall by dropping him from the doubles in favour of Hartwig. In any case, the plan backfired, with Australia losing the doubles; and any hope of retaining the cup rested with Hoad and Rosewall in the reverse singles. Again, Hoad was equal to the situation, overcoming Trabert to bring the series to 2-all. This too was Rosewall's finest hour, in defeating Seixas in four sets to win one of the most dramatic ties of the post-war era.

Hoad and Rosewall continued their Davis Cup involvement until

1956, which saw a mix of fortunes for Australia, with the cup returning to The United States in 1954. Australia's fortunes were elevated with its return to our shores in 1955 and with another win in 1956. Throughout that period Hoad and Rosewall were key members of the squad until the end of 1956 when Rosewall made a not-unexpected move to the professional ranks.

In 1957 Hoad made a similar decision. The Australian tennis public was genuinely upset with their departure from the amateur game, which proved to be the natural progression for our leading players over the ensuing years. Rosewall's professional career extended over a remarkable twenty four years, until his eventual retirement around 1980. During that stellar period he won 23 Majors, including eight Grand Slam singles titles, and before the Open era a record 15 Pro-slam titles. In Jack Kramer's estimation, Rosewall deserved to be included in his list of the 21 greatest players of all time. His outstanding record was also recognised in Australia's New Year's Honours with the award of the A.M. (Australia Medal) and the MBE (Member of the British Empire). In a well-earned retirement Ken Rosewall lives in northern Sydney, where he still frequently plays tennis.

Ken Kavanagh, Aussie racing legend

Ken Kavanagh's racing forays were typical of the Australian riders who made the pilgrimage to Europe in the early 1950s. Veterans, Harry Hinton and Eric McPherson who preceded him both earned World Championship points and also secured works rides. Kavanagh was determined to make his mark in Grand Prix racing and succeeded far beyond his contemporaries. During his career he gained works rides from four manufacturers; Norton, Moto Guzzi, MV and Ducati.

Kavanagh was the first Australian to win a classic Grand Prix and to also win at the Isle of Man; in his case, the 1953 Senior Ulster and the 1956 Junior TT. His competition career began in motocross or scrambles as it was known in Australia. He moved from there to road racing, riding a new Manx Norton; the first to be imported post war to Australia. Kavanagh became the man to beat in Victorian road races. His big opportunity came in 1951 when he was chosen for the Isle of Man team, partnering Harry Hinton and Tony McAlpine.

The TT was Kavanagh's main focus on his arrival in Europe. He applied himself to learning that complex 37-mile circuit in a disciplined manner, with fast lap times and without the ignominy of crashing.

A feature of Kavanagh's career was his ability to avoid dropping the model. These were times when many of the circuits were incredibly dangerous, with no run-off areas and road conditions that would be quite unacceptable today. Under such circumstances there were inevitable fatalities, including many aspiring Australian riders.

Kavanagh was actually offered a works Norton for the Senior TT.

Hinton's injury in the Junior TT left the team one rider short and it was a rare compliment for Kavanagh, on his first Island foray. He rejected the offer, saying that his own Manx Nortons were quick enough for his current experience. During the Senior TT he worked his way into fourth place, only to retire with a split oil tank.

Following the TT Kavanagh scored his first ever-European victory with a win in a 500cc race at the Thruxton circuit. He was also successful at the Tarare circuit in France, winning the 350 and 500 races. Other wins followed his French outings and for the Ulster Grand Prix he was enlisted into the Norton team alongside Geoff Duke, Johnnie Lockett and Jack Brett. Kavanagh justified his inclusion with a strong second place to Duke in both the 350 and 500cc events.

Kavanagh returned to Australia in October, following a superb performance by a newcomer to European racing. Back in England for the 1952 season he scored 350 and 500cc wins at Boreham Wood, making him a British Champion. His Isle of Man Senior outing, like the previous year proved disappointing. He was holding fourth place on the final lap when his primary chain broke. Determined to finish he pushed and coasted the final six miles to come 32nd. His Junior TT resulted in retirement with mechanical problems, again while holding 4th place. It was a season of mixed fortunes for the 1952 Norton team.

At the German Grand prix on the Solitude road circuit Ray Amm crashed in practice, sustaining a broken leg and other injuries. Team leader Duke was also absent, following a crash at Schotten on the previous weekend. It was left to Kavanagh and Armstrong to uphold Norton's honour. Kavanagh was poised to win the 350 race only to have Armstrong beat him to the line by a wheel's length.

His Senior race was an example of riding to team orders. In his efforts to keep ahead of Graham's MV, Kavanagh built up an adequate lead over the MV and Armstrong's Norton. Graham encountered problems, putting Armstrong into second place. At the time Armstrong held a slender lead in the 500cc World Championship, making it imperative that Kavanagh surrender his first place. He duly slowed his pace to allow Armstrong to come through for his second win of the day. That year's Ulster Grand Prix brought a more satisfying result for the Australian with first place ahead of Armstrong in the 350 event. It was the final year that the GP was held on the old Clady circuit, prior to its move to Dundrod.

Armstrong needed a win in the 500 race to consolidate his narrow points lead in the World Championship but he was forced to retire with a broken chain. It was an exasperating occurrence that bedevilled Nortons on so many occasions. Cromie McCandless won the Senior, riding a work's Gilera.

For 1953 Kavanagh was once more a Norton teamster alongside Ray Amm and Jack Brett. Geoff Duke and Reg Armstrong had moved to Gilera, following an unprofitable season for them on Nortons. Despite the speed advantage of the Italian fours the Norton's superior handling kept them competitive at tortuous circuits like the Isle of Man. Kavanagh was confident of a good result at the Junior TT and came tantalizingly close to achieving that win.

On lap four he assumed the lead, ousting early leader Ray Amm. The Rhodesian was in tigerish mood and not to be denied. By dint of a record-breaking final lap he came through to beat Kavanagh by the margin of just nine seconds! Friday's Senior TT was even more dramatic for Amm. Following Les Graham's fatal crash on lap 2 Amm held second place behind Duke's Gilera. Then on lap 3 Duke came off at Quarter Bridge, damaging the Gilera too seriously to continue. Amm took over in first place, holding it till the finish with a record lap at 97.41 mph.

Early in the race Kavanagh was well in the picture, climbing to fourth place by lap 3 only to retire shortly afterwards. Duke's move to Gilera was clearly vindicated with wins at the 500cc Dutch TT and the Swiss and Italian Grands Prix. Kavanagh secured 4th place at the 500 Belgian GP, however the 500 Ulster Grand Prix was his moment of triumph. He was hoping for a leader board finish behind the Gileras until fate took a hand with torrential rain and clutch problems with Duke's Gilera. Midway through the race Kavanagh took over the lead while Duke was refuelling. Riding as never before in the rain-lashed conditions he held on to score a memorable win and become the first Australian to win a classic Grand Prix.

Kavanagh's final appearance on a work's Norton was an end-of-season meeting at Silverstone. It was a circuit he disliked, due to its use for car racing which left the surface absolutely without grip. He was untroubled to win the 350 race while the 500 final was a much more demanding exercise. Kavanagh was slipstreaming Dale's Gilera when he was brought down by the Gilera suddenly locking up. The Aussie was soon on his way again, regaining the lead to score his last win for the firm.

From 1954 to 1957 Kavanagh was retained as a works rider for Moto Guzzi. It was a productive era for the diminutive Australian with wins at the 1954 350 Belgian GP, the 1955 350 Dutch TT and a strong third place in the 1955 Senior TT behind Duke and Armstrong's Gileras. More significantly he won the 1956 Isle of Man Junior TT, becoming the first Australian to attain victory at a venue where good fortune rarely smiled on Thomas Kenrick Kavanagh.

His fellow riders were divided in their opinion of Kavanagh. Some considered his forceful ambition and total commitment as unsavoury. Without doubt he secured deals that made him the most successful of his contemporaries by far. Much of his wealth was lost in a foray into Formula One during 1958 and 1959. He was acquired a pair of ex-works lightweight Maserati 250Fs. His partner in the venture was fellow Aussie Keith Campbell, sadly the former 350cc world champion was killed at a minor race meeting at Cadours early in 1958. Motor racing soaks up a private entrant's funds at an alarming rate, as Kavanagh and many others found, to their cost. After two unproductive seasons he abandoned the exercise.

In 1959 he made a return to two wheels with race entries on Nortons, the make on which his career began. He also campaigned Ducatis in the 125 and 250 categories. By then the Japanese influence was being extended into road racing. It was an invasion that Kavanagh resented, and on that note Kavanagh retired. He abandoned his Australian connections and settled in the northern Italian town of Bergamo. There he operated a dry cleaning business, a far cry from the glamour and excitement of his Grand Prix racing days.

W/Cdr. Hughie Edwards

With the fall of France in July 1940, Western Europe, apart from Spain and Portugal fell under Nazi subjugation. Great Britain finally stood alone to face the anticipated Battle of Britain, to be followed by 'Operation Sea Lion', the projected seaborne invasion of the British Isles. Although vastly inferior in numbers to a rampant Luftwaffe, RAF Fighter Command would emerge triumphant from that dramatic encounter, arguably the most decisive battle of the twentieth century.

Throughout that turbulent, early phase of World War 2, RAF Bomber Command offered the one opportunity to carry the offensive into the Nazi aggressor's domain. Despite the daunting casualty rate, Australia provided Bomber Command with some notable airmen; not the least of these was Hughie Idwal Edwards.

The future Air Commodore and VC winner was born in Western Australia in 1914 of a Welsh immigrant family. His determination to pursue an aviation career was realised in 1936 with his acceptance as a cadet in the Royal Australian Air Force. To further his career, in 1938 he transferred to the Royal Air Force, where he continued his training on the newly-introduced Bristol Blenheim.

In the course of a training flight Edwards was forced to make an emergency bailout, and had the misfortune to strike the aircraft's tailplane and suffer severe damage to his leg. That situation was further aggravated in the ensuing heavy parachute landing. So severe was the problem that his flying career appeared to be finished. However, by determination and persistence with medical boards he finally achieved a full flying category.

During a night-flying exercise in 1940 Edwards suffered a further setback; when a Luftwaffe raid in his sector forced the closure of local airfields and total radio silence. He elected to remain with his aircraft and face the daunting prospect of a forced landing in a blacked-out countryside. In a collision with a large tree Edwards suffered severe concussion, a factor that prevented him from becoming operational until early 1941.

His posting to 105 squadron in Norfolk coincided with a period of maximum effort of daylight raids on shipping and heavily defended objectives in occupied Europe. At that stage of the war the Blenheims of No.2 Group were approaching obsolescence and suffering heavy operational losses, nevertheless operations continued unabated.

Edwards was awarded the DFC during that period and attained the rank of acting wing commander, due to losses and his own fortuitous survival. Germany had invaded Russia in June 1941 and to draw elements of the Luftwaffe from the Eastern Front the British War Council began a policy of heavier attacks on German-occupied territory.

On July 4, units from No.2 Group were ordered to carry out a significant raid on the port of Bremen in northern Germany. This followed a night attack from Bomber Command on the previous evening. Edwards was chosen to lead the risky daylight mission; comprising a combined force of nine Blenheims from 105 squadron and six from 107. He led the formation at wave level over the North Sea and as they neared the target he made a turn to the northeast. His plan was to approach Bremen from a northerly direction in the hope they might achieve an element of surprise,

However, Bremen's defences were fully alerted as the Blenheims swept in, lined out in
single file; with each pilot selecting an individual target. The formation ran the gauntlet of barrage balloons and vicious flak, heavy enough to

account for two aircraft that were brought down over the target while another turned inland and failed to link up with the formation. Considerable damage was inflicted on the dock area and warehouses, after which Edwards skilfully marshalled his forces and led them home with no further loss

A fortnight later; following the Bremen raid Edwards was awarded the Victoria Cross, the first to an Australian airman in World War 2, the citation of which concluded:

> 'Throughout the execution of this operation, which he had planned personally with full knowledge of the risks entailed, Wing Commander Edwards displayed the highest possible standard of gallantry and determination.'

In a gesture of appreciation Edwards framed the citation and presented it to the squadron, maintaining that the award was a team effort and not an individual one. Shortly afterwards the squadron was posted to a beleaguered Malta where it operated on shipping strikes and once again Edwards survived his tour despite the inevitable heavy losses.

On his return to the U.K. he was selected to accompany a group of RAF commanders on a goodwill tour of The United States and Canada. In December he was operational again with 105, which had replaced its obsolete Blenheims with De Havilland Mosquitoes; the first RAF squadron to operate with this exceptional aircraft. On 6 December 1942 he led a combined force of Mosquito, Boston and Ventura bombers on Operation Oyster, a large-scale daylight raid on the Philips electrical factory at Eindhoven in Holland.

RAF losses were heavy, with 14 aircraft brought down by flak and fighters. Damage to the factory was substantial, while few casualties were suffered by Dutch workers. Edward's leadership on this and other missions was recognised with the award of the DSO. Following this was his tenure as Station Commander at RAF, Binbrook, and home base for the celebrated No 460 Lancaster squadron (RAAF) of No.1 Group.

Despite the administrative duties of the command Edwards carried out a number night operations himself.

In December 1944 he was promoted to Group Captain and posted to South East Asia Command where he occupied various senior posts. He remained in the Command until 1947, returning to the United Kingdom to attend the RAF Staff College. Edwards returned to flying duties in 1950 and between 1953 and 1956 commanded a jet fighter base before being posted to Iraq for a three- year term as station commander of the RAF Base at Habbaniyah.

Edwards was accorded further promotions and honours; notably as Air Commodore and Commandant of the Flying Wing at RAF Brize Norton until his retirement from the Royal Air Force in September 1963. Edwards returned to Western Australia and began a successful business career. In 1974 he was knighted and appointed Governor of Western Australia. It was a position that he was forced to resign the following year due to ill health.

In company with former squadron companion and Test cricketer Keith Miller, Edwards was about to attend a match at Sydney Cricket Ground in 1982 when he unexpectedly collapsed and died, aged 68. Hughie Edwards was a remarkable warrior, the most highly decorated Australian of World War 2 and one of the giants of Bomber Command; deservedly remembered alongside Guy Gibson, Leonard Cheshire, Donald Bennett and a host of other luminaries.

(An excerpt from 'For Valour')

Pacific Conquest 1928

'First across the Pacific'. That was the burning ambition of ex-RFC pilots, Charles Kingsford Smith and Keith Anderson. In Western Australia in the early 1920s they operated an aerial taxi service and later a road haulage business. In 1927 the partners moved to Sydney where they hoped to find local air charter work. That particular venture was unsuccessful but a meeting occurred with a third party, which had a profound effect on their fortunes. Charles Ulm had no piloting skills; instead his talents lay in organizing, which he pursued in a ruthless, unwavering manner. Anderson was of an easy-going nature and soon found himself relegated to the background by the thrusting, single-minded Ulm.

In an attempt to gain sponsorship for the Pacific flight, Smithy and Ulm embarked on around-Australia flight using one of Smithy's elderly Bristol Tourers. Their circumnavigation was completed in a record 10 days, which created favourable responses from various sources. Confident that the financial problems were covered, the trio boarded a steamer for The United States in July 1927 to prepare for the Pacific flight. Shortly after their arrival they were able to purchase an aircraft suitable for their requirements from Polar explorer Hubert Wilkins. It was a Fokker FV11 B tri-motor, one of a pair that Wilkins had used on a recent Polar flight. Unfortunately the Fokker, which they named 'Southern Cross' came without motors and instruments. These were beyond their funds, but with an additional £1,000 from the NSW Government and a further £1,500 from Melbourne businessman,

Sydney Myer the project gained momentum. 'Southern Cross' was then fitted out with three Wright Whirlwind motors, instruments and long-range tanks, but the partners' money was fast running out. With the situation becoming desperate, Anderson returned to Australia, convinced that the project had no future.

Smithy and Ulm were basically destitute and burdened with debts that amounted to $16,000. Reluctantly they made the decision to sell the Fokker and return to Sydney. In a stroke of good fortune their financial problems were solved by the intervention of millionaire banker, Alan Hancock. This quiet businessman was also an experienced marine navigator with a great interest in aviation. He was sufficiently impressed with the Australians to take over their sizeable debts and fund the Pacific flight. Two Americans were recruited to complete the crew; Harry Lyon, former ship's captain and a superb navigator, and James Warner, a radio operator with many years service with the U.S. Navy and Merchant Marine.

It was Smithy's moment of destiny. For years his obsession was the Pacific flight, and after incredible setbacks it was about to be realized. It also carried a bitter irony for Anderson; being denied his opportunity to be part of the team. On the last day of May 1928 the grossly overladen 'Southern Cross' lifted off from San Francisco's Oakland airport. Their take-off was the most critical stage of the flight, so laden with fuel their speed was barely above the stall. It was a situation they faced for several hours until enough fuel was burned for them to gain precious altitude. Communication between navigator and pilot was achieved by way of notes pushed through a tube that ran from rear cabin to cockpit. Engine noise was so intrusive that conversation between pilot and co-pilot was impossible. They too were compelled to resort to scribbled notes to each other. Their first stage of the journey they were blessed with ideal weather conditions; clear and sunny and with the bonus of a tail wind. Twenty-four hours into the flight they were faced with a crisis when the batteries for the receiver and transmitter expired, making it absolutely vital that Lyon's navigation was faultless. Several times land was sighted, but to their disappointment the sightings proved to be cloud masses. Warner received a reassuring signal from a shore station giving them an indication of their position. At the same time Lyon managed to obtain an accurate sun shot that verified the signal. For another hour 'Southern Cross' cruised above heavy cloud while the crew watched anxiously for a long-overdue sighting of land. It became a race against the possibility of running out of fuel and a landfall.

At last they were rewarded with the sight of the 14,000 feet volcano, Mauna Kea on Hawaii Island; Lyon's navigation had been impeccable. Sixty minutes later they landed at Wheeler Field at Honolulu to complete the 2,300-mile crossing in 27 hours 30 minutes.

Following the euphoria of the first leg, 'Southern Cross' and its crew faced the most critical stage of the journey; 3,150 miles to Fiji and the first ever attempt by air. Smithy chose a beach at Barking Sands on the outer island of Kauai for the take-off. In retrospect it bordered on the suicidal with the all-up weight dangerously close to the aircraft's limits. It was a nerve-wracking experience for its crew and for the spectators. They watched in trepidation as 'Southern Cross' staggered into the air with its landing wheels skimming the waves as Smithy kept it airborne. It was some time before they clawed their way to an altitude of 500 feet and received assistance from a helpful tail wind. Three hours into the flight the troublesome radio problems returned, leaving them with only the capacity to transmit messages. Around mid-day they hit the inter-tropical convergence zone, an area host to storms of extreme ferocity.

Menacing clouds exploded with thunder and lightning, rising to altitudes of 35,000 feet; and making it quite impossible to fly over. 'Southern Cross' plunged into the boiling mass where it was flung about like a leaf in a storm. All of Smithy's skills were needed to keep it airborne, in conditions that were akin to flying through a waterfall that drenched the pilots from head to foot. At one stage the aircraft was almost flipped upside down, so severe was the turbulence.

Eventually they emerged into clear skies, and by Lyon's reckoning they had covered over 1,000 miles, almost one third of the distance. To their horror they saw ahead of them another threatening cloud mass, hundreds of miles across. Once more it became a desperate battle against the elements as Smithy endeavoured to climb above the worst of it; and after three terrifying hours they emerged into a moonlit starry night. According to Lyon they were 1,100 miles from Fiji and with 500 gallons of fuel remaining. By Smithy's calculations that was inadequate, which meant they might have to find an alternative island for a set-down. The remaining hours until daylight dragged by in an atmosphere of tension and when the time came to hand pump the remaining fuel they discovered there was ample to cover the distance.

Lyon was able to obtain a shot of the sun during the morning, which showed they were north of their intended course. It was a tribute to his navigation after the constant detours during those violent storms and without a single radio bearing from ship or shore to assist him. 'Southern Cross' arrived over Suva in the early afternoon and Smithy wasn't impressed with the miniscule landing ground at Albert Park. He made a search for a suitable beach as an alternative but they were even less promising; it had to be Albert Park. An enormous crowd had gathered to witness their arrival. they were privileged to see Smithy perform a masterly landing in the confined space.

Just when it seemed 'Southern Cross' was about to career into some large trees Smithy swung away in a spectacular ground loop. The Americans were crouched in the rear of the fuselage in an endeavour to hold down the tail of the aircraft. During the violent landing the unfortunate Warner was flung through the fabric and knocked unconscious. He was fortunate not to be run over, and after being rendered first aid he quickly recovered. For the final leg to Brisbane Smithy used Naselau Beach from where they took off on Friday 8 June. Being a far shorter flight; a maximum fuel load was deemed unnecessary. As they headed into a brilliant clear sky, crewmembers were quietly confident they were almost home. With the difficult part of the journey behind them they could hardly miss a target the size of Australia.

Their euphoria was dealt a severe blow when soon after nightfall they flew into an electrical storm of terrifying proportions. All of Smithy's blind- flying skills were called on to keep 'Southern Cross' airborne. In an attempt to find a more favourable situation they climbed to 9,000 feet, where they faced bitterly cold conditions.

Even at that altitude the Fokker was forced up and down in alarming surges. In the rudimentary cockpit the pilots were flung out of their seats as they clung desperately to the control wheels. For the Americans they fared even worse in conditions that at times rendered them weightless. During the five hours of their ordeal it was impossible for Lyon to navigate and when they did emerge from the storm he estimated they were at least 100 miles off course. It was fortunate their goal was Australia and not a speck in the ocean like Fiji. Around 8am a shadow appeared on the horizon, which according to Lyon was the coast of northern New South Wales. Smithy identified it as Ballina, 110 miles south of Brisbane. An error of that magnitude on the Fiji leg did not bear consideration.

As they neared Brisbane, 'Southern Cross' was welcomed by a flight of light aircraft. At 10.15 a.m. Smithy made a textbook landing at Eagle Farm aerodrome. It would be difficult to put a precise number to the crowd that had waited since 3am. That figure varied from 15,000 to 40,000 but there was no doubting their adulation for the crew. Smithy became the centre of attraction as women attempted to smother him with kisses while men fought to shake his hand. It was the beginning of an era of pop-idol fame for the effervescent Aussie. Their flight statistics showed they had covered 7,220 miles in eight and a half days and in a flying time of 83 hours. Present day travellers might take a moment to compare their journey in the pressurized ease of a 747 Jumbo to the acute discomfort and appalling danger of that Pacific crossing of 1928.

Matthew Glenn Ward

Matthew Glenn Ward could talk underwater and has probably tried to. His mind is mercurial and always moving, like ripples on a lake. He's nocturnal, day-urnal and any-urnal he can be, but as a professional he is a masterful, organised, presenter of workshops.
www.matthewglennward.com

The Great Homework Swindle

Time takes an eternity when you're 12. Especially when you take a day off school. Not doing homework in the late 1970s meant sore hands and wounded pride, and those suffering such indignities never seemed to learn. I was one of those occasional homework defaulters and my plan of 'wopping' school as we called it seemed a good one at 8am on the morning the Mathematics homework was due.

Anyway, some back story. In 1979 I was in my first year of high school at the old St Pius X College Adamstown (Newcastle NSW Australia). The older, white building with the zig-zag roof used to be an underwear factory in the 1950s where my mum used to work as a clerk. I believe in the 1960s it was sold to the Catholic Church and there they established St Pius X College, an all boys secondary school that only admitted girls in the mid-1980s. Chattering sewing machines were replaced with priests, desks, blackboards, crucifixes and chattering students.

I had an uncle who attended 'Pius' in the '60s, but most of the males in my family went to Marist Brothers Hamilton, in 'Town' as we called inner city Newcastle (and still do). But we lived in New Lambton, a lot closer to Pius than 'Marist' so when given the choice of schools I chose Pius, mainly because of distance.

Maths was never my signature event. English, History, even Science came easy to me but the mystery of numbers always baffled me because I had to *try* and I was lazy. And because I was lazy I would conveniently 'forget' to do homework related to certain subjects I couldn't stand.

Maths was one of those subjects.

So one cold Newcastle morning I packed up my black sports bag with books and headed not to the bottom field entrance of the college but instead to the corner store on the Bridges Road side of Alder Park to wait until that Maths class was over. My theory was that the homework would be dealt with by our teacher Mr Ron 'Lefty' Wright and I would not have to do it.

The little shop was called 'Louie's' by everyone we knew. It was run by a kind man of European extraction called Louie. The name 'Nantsou' was painted on the wall out front so I gathered his name was Louie Nantsou. Made sense to me even at that young age. My nan, when she lived in New Lambton about a quarter of a kay away, used to send me on errands to buy the essentials: bread, butter, milk, sometimes Devon, and also Benson & Hedges cigarettes. She used to call Louie up to tell him I was on my way. I'd hand over a $10 paper bill and Louie would hand me the groceries.

Back in 1979 one could get a small bottle of Coke or Fanta for 17 cents, believe it or not. So on this crisp morning at 8am I walked into Louie's shop, bought a small bottle of Fanta and sat down on a cold, metal fold-up promotional Coke chair. I slowly sipped the Fanta, and glanced every now and then at my 9th birthday Lauris watch. Class started at 9am. History was first (with teacher, Mr Smyth, a former Spitfire pilot). Then Geography (Mr Mulconry). Finally Maths. So that was 2 and a half hours for me to wait!

I chatted with Louie about business (as if I knew what I was talking about). I might have bought a second bottle of drink, (I cannot remember). I would have looked at the array of canned goods on the shelves, the customers who walked in and out, and the traffic that bounded up Bridges Road towards the old Garden City shopping centre in Kotara. Finally, I left, thanking Louie on my way out.

I dawdled back along the road, past Alder Park Bowling Club, the old Caltex service station, under the overhead train bridge, through the gate and across the bottom football field. I ambled across the stormwater canal bridge, looked up and was surprised to see boys out playing when they still should have been in class.

I saw one of my friends and he asked me where I was. I made something up, like I was sick. I asked him why everyone was out of class and he said that because of the sports carnival later in the week, the timetable was changed to Tuesday's, and they were having an early lunch. (The Maths class I was hoping to miss didn't even happen.)

When I did go to the next Maths class, a few days later (my mind is hazy on this but I believe) I cobbled together something in the way of homework to show the teacher, but he had forgotten and we moved on to something else.

Missing the Newcastle Earthquake

Before the earthquake of 1989, Newcastle NSW was known as a 'large industrial town.' After the earthquake of 1989 Newcastle NSW was known as 'that large industrial town that had an earthquake'. In the twenty years since the earthquake, she has since become less of an industrial town and a little bit closer to a modern, bohemian city whose population used to remember the natural disaster every year, but now only does so every five or ten years.

What I hated was I was not in my home town when the earthquake hit. I was in Coffs Harbour on holiday with my younger brother, Philip; a mate, Tony; and my brother's mate, Darren. This is how it all went down. At the then mature age of 23, I was 'absent without leave' when my city had its biggest event since the flaming car Star Hotel riots of 1979 that shortly after was immortalised by Aussie rockers Cold Chisel.

We'd crept into a Coffs Harbour caravan park around mid-afternoon on December 27th 1989, tired after Christmas and Boxing Day celebrations, and a little jetlagged by the trip from Newcastle—a jetlagged feeling even though we travelled there by car, if that makes any sense.

We constructed a slipshod tent and I crashed in there immediately despite the hot weather. To my confusion, I awoke an hour later in the orange light to the sound of giggling and the sight of a little green crab that was inching itself towards me, pincers ready—I believed—to sever my little toes. The giggling was not the crab, as you might have gathered, but the other guys outside who did this sort of thing for a lark all the time, as we all did.

That night we walked from the caravan park in our going to town clothes, my then long hair split-enzy because I used Sunlight Soap instead of shampoo in the caravan shower block. Anyway, at a club we drank expensive watered down scotches and Cokes, watched music videos on a big screen and then hours later walked back to the caravan park with that 'paid too much to not to get anywhere' feeling.

Next morning on December 28th we woke up around 9am, dressed casually and shortly after went by car into town to grab breakfast. On the way back, Darren, who was driving, decided to bunny hop his car around another caravan park. Inevitably the clutch cable snapped. We then pushed the car in the heat to the local Mitsubishi parts place, the rest of us hoping that this example of buffoonery would cost Darren a motza. It didn't. He wasn't called Lucky the Cat for nothing. The clutch cable for his model of Sigma, a GE (1978), was only $20 or something. The models after the GE had cables that started at over $100.

So, being someone who worked in the car game I knew that even though Darren would be paying next to nothing for his cable, they wouldn't have one for at least a week—it might even have to come from Japan—and then he'd have to book in to get it done. Well, they had one and said they could fix it within the hour for next to nothing. Lucky the Cat strikes again.

After the car was roadworthy once more, we cruised to get lunch in the middle of Coffs. Strange things then started to happen. I went to an autoteller and was told via an onscreen message that the bank I was trying to get money from, The Newcastle Permanent, was down. Then we got back into the car and just drove around. Someone put the car radio on. There was some music and we chatted generally about nothing in particular just as the DJ said: 'And we'll give you more info on the Newcastle earthquake as it comes to hand...' Someone in the car told the others to shut up, and we waited an eternity for the DJ to get back to us. We assumed the whole thing was a joke as he played

Martika's then popular cover of Carole King's 'I Feel the Earth Move'.

We all decided we had to be back in Newcastle, so we went back to the caravan park to pack. Tony and I hung around waiting for Philip and Darren and we met an old man who told us the best place to go for a bite was the RSL where we could get a baked dinner and 'exotic things like peas and carrots and potatoes'. We knew all about peas, carrots and potatoes but let him talk as he seemed to delight in telling us the marvels of baked dinners.

So, we travelled in two cars, Darren driving his car with Philip as shotgun, and Tony driving his brown metallic V8 HZ Kingswood with me in the passenger seat, both vehicles trying to get to Newcastle as quickly as possible but Tony winning due to sheer horsepower.

Tony and I eventually arrived back in Newcastle after lunch, eager to go cruise Main and see what the damage was, from Hamilton where awnings had collapsed on cars and the Newcastle Worker's Club where poker machine playing pensioners had shuffled through dust and spilled coins to try and escape the rubble of the floor.

Trouble was every stickybeak Novocastrian and rubbernecker from outside Newcastle was determined to get into Newcastle as well. The roads all the way back were packed. We sat in the car outside Wickham Gates for an eternity. We had to have a story ready as security was only allowing certain people through, turning most away who u-turned it back to where they came from. We cooked up a half-baked story that I had a brother in Merewether and was concerned for his welfare. I gave the story to the security guy and he asked where my brother lived. We hadn't thought that far ahead, and he gave us the 'good try' look and urged us to turn around, which we did. Traffic was thick going back to the suburbs, but eventually I arrived home to New Lambton while Tony left to see his family in Kotara.

My brother arrived soon after, and we relayed our stories to our parents and my younger sister who had escaped from Newcastle an hour or so before from her workplace, Spotlight, a retailer of manchester, fabric etc. My parents were worried after hearing apocalyptic stories on the radio of Newcastle totally collapsing and greeted her with relief.

When the quake happened, everyone in my street apparently went outside, not having ever been prepared for such a natural disaster. It didn't hit anywhere near as badly as in the city but still it had been a shock. When I heard this I wished I had been there, too.

News stories of the after-effects were ever-present on the media and on the streets. Novocastrians loved talking about the tragedy. Unfortunately, several people lost their lives and we watched stories on TV of relatives of the deceased reliving their stories of woe.

In the following week, the Newcastle CBD and Hamilton were turned into ghost towns, with only those who owned buildings that were deemed safe or tradesmen allowed to enter the zones. Tony was a plumber at the time and was called in to do work, so he kept the rest of us updated on the situation in town.

Being an avid amateur photographer, the following week I travelled over in my car to Tighes Hill, a suburb next to Hamilton, which had had its own shakeup. That year I had been going part-time to tech (TAFE) and I was keen to see if it had sustained any damage. It had, and I used my zoom lens SLR to photograph fallen walls, and red & white taped off areas. I also talked to some teachers who were not allowed into their workplace until they were given the okay, which was at least a week away.

A week after that, buildings started to get demolished. In Tighes Hill I stood with 50 or so curious onlookers, a lot with cameras, while a pub was knocked down. In New Lambton similar crowds gathered as the facade of the pharmacy in Orchard town Road was toppled over. The old George Hotel in town, where my Nan had worked in the '70s, was apparently too unstable and had to be knocked down, yet when they tried she held on, refusing to go, and those of us who used to go there as underage drinkers with fake photocopied boat licenses were very proud of her steadfastedness that day.

Scenes like this were repeated all over the city and suburbs. The excitement then died down and thousands of people whose homes had been damaged by the earthquake struggled to get their abodes habitable again. Some of them would wait years.

A few years later I was at university. One afternoon I was at home talking on the phone to my friend Michelle. The sliding door to my room was closed, then someone rattled it to say, I assumed, that dinner was ready or that someone was at the door to see me.

'Yeah, hang on,' I yelled out.

Michelle said: 'What in the f*** was that?'

'What was what?' I replied.

'I think that was a tremor,' she said.

'Cool,' I said, I wasn't here for the last one (in 1989).'

'Well I was,' she said. 'I'm getting outa here!'

'No, just stand under the doorframe,' I said and did just that (I had read that somewhere).

Well, she uttered something unprintable and rushed outside her flat and into the street.

It's interesting to note that at the time of the turmoil in Newcastle, where we were in Coffs Harbour was very quiet, peaceful. Tony and I had been sitting on grass in the caravan park playing chess, while in our home town of Newcastle, people ran for their lives. I can't remember who won that chess game but that doesn't matter, does it? While we were playing a peaceful game that represented war, while a peaceful city was in the midst of its own war, against nature.

Years after the earthquake, when Novocastrians told their tales, I had always felt left out, but I was soon warmed by the curiosity of others who wanted to know about my time in Coffs at the time of the quake, the very story you are reading now. It was still an earthquake story, I realised, and as relevant as any other earthquake story.

A Labrador goes shopping! ~

When I was a boy living in my home town of Newcastle, NSW, my constant companion was a Labrador Retriever named Caesar. In the 1970s all dogs seemed to have been named after kings, like Caesar, Kaiser, Rex, or... King. He arrived as an 8 month old youngster on our doorstep when we lived in Ipswich Queensland.

I was about five at the time. Caesar had belonged to another family and they gave him to us. I believe it was because they lived somewhere where they weren't allowed to have pets. My dad was in the Air Force and in 1974 he was transferred to Newcastle, and our dog came with us.

Caesar was walked every day by my father and, when I was old enough to go to the park by myself, around the age of 9, I would take Caesar with me, let him off the leash when we arrived at the park, then tie him up again and walk him home where he always hurriedly slurped down a dog dish full of water.

Most of the time he was kept in our large back yard. My parents were scared if they let him roam the streets he might end up in the local pound or run over on the road. He seemed content with this for the first few years until he found out he could escape over the fence at night, wander around the local bushland for hours on end, and return in the early hours of the morning.

No-one would have been the wiser, had he not reeked to high heaven of the tossed garbage bags he'd nuzzle through, and sported a tide mark along his belly showing he'd been swimming in ponds, no doubt trying and failing to get his paws on local wildlife (more on that practice later).

During the day Caesar would laze around like other dogs, occasionally going for a drink of water around the back of the house, or sitting in the sun while my mum would hang out the clothes on the 1950's style fence-to-fence clothesline.

Then, at about 3:00pm every day he'd instinctively get up and make his way either over the fence, or if it was open, through one of the side gates and up the street where he'd sit on the footpath, looking down the hill waiting for the school bus that would carry my younger brother, sister and me home.

Then, after the bus would depart, he'd stand and stare at the vaguely recognizable children in the distance, waiting for us to get closer. Then we'd call out his name and he'd come running, his ham tongue dripping saliva down those black rubber-like gums to the tar road. We'd greet him, pat his head and he'd accompany us home where we'd get afternoon sandwiches and cordial from Mum, and watch TV.

Occasionally, just to gently tease him, we'd get off the bus at the next stop, creep around the corner, wait until he was watching the other way, and make it to our front fence by hiding behind nature strip trees. He'd be confused that we hadn't jumped off the bus, but then he'd be relieved when we called out his name. The race up the stairs to the front door was always a close one with one happy Labrador right on our tails.

Back in Queensland, Caesar had been a bit of a handful, although one had to see the humour in the predicaments he found himself in. Once, he disappeared for a day until my dad received a phone call, asking if he owned a golden Labrador. My dad said yes, and then jumped in the car to go pick up this juvenile delinquent who had met up with a more experienced black Labrador earlier that day and decided to chase some chickens. Dad found Caesar tied up, feeling very sorry for himself. The man who called said the other dog was probably the ringleader, and Caesar the gullible sidekick.

Then, there was fun with my mother driving the family car. One day she was learning to drive - and this was about 1973 - with the driving school instructor sitting in the passenger seat and as she drove the streets of Eastern Heights, Ipswich, she happened to glance in her rear vision mirror to see a very tired looking dog running behind her. She pulled over to the side of the road and saw, to her alarm, our dog's paws worn down so much they were bleeding.

The car wasn't hers and she thought our dog would make a mess on the back seat, so she turned the car around and drove slowly back, allowing Caesar a leisurely hobble back home to where his feet were treated with something soothing like Rawleigh's 'Antiseptic Salve' or lanolin.

When we moved to Newcastle in 1974 my mum didn't often drive, but one day Caesar saw her driving a few streets away from home. He thought he'd surprise her by jumping through the driver's door window right onto her lap! Trouble was the car wasn't ours, and the woman wasn't my mother. Our dog had a puzzled look on his face as the woman quite understandably screamed in panic.

When I was about 13 I used to walk over to Garden City Kotara, the local shopping centre (now called Westfield Kotara) with a mate of mine, Bill. We didn't have much money in those days, usually enough for a drink, some chips or a few cinnamon donuts, but we liked to go the record shop, called The Green Apple, and also to look at bikes at Norman Ross.

Getting away from the house without Caesar seeing us and following was a difficult one; even my mother if she went out in the day on errands, would be quiet when she shut and locked the front door as our loyal dog would hear her, start whimpering, then bound over the fence and 'walk her' down to the bus stop.

One day he followed my brother and me down to the bus stop and jumped right on the bus with us, much to the amusement of the other kids on the bus. He was ordered off by me, the door shut and the bus took off, the dog running for a 100 metres or so before he tired and the bus was out of sight.

One Thursday night, the traditional late shopping night, Bill and I grabbed around $5.00 each and trotted off to Garden City. Two streets away from home, I could hear a dog's feet padding the road, and panting. You guessed it, Caesar had decided we needed company.

I was afraid he would get run over so I ordered him home. I'd point homeward, yell: 'No! Go home!' He'd look in the direction of the finger, look back to smile and then pant. No matter what I did he wouldn't listen. So he came with us.

In a moment of impetuous foolishness I decided to split from him when we arrived at Garden City. I thought he'd just stay out the front on the grass and we could gather him on our way home a couple of hours later. I told him to stay. He didn't. I told him to go home. He wouldn't. He just followed us into the centre like he was our brother.

So, there we were, two 13 year old boys and a Labrador walking through Garden City Kotara with everyone staring at us. (It was so embarrassing for me at that fragile age.) We walked into the David Jones store. It was there that we finally lost Caesar when we jumped on the Up escalator. Caesar had never seen moving stairs before and just stood looking up at me as I disappeared.

Bill and I went around the top floor and took our time looking at stereos, watching TV, checking out sports equipment, and generally having a good time. We were away maybe 20 minutes and then we rode the down escalator when we soon heard loud, mournful howling. It was Caesar, at the base of the escalator, still waiting for me and surrounding him were three or four very attractive David Jones' girls, trying to console my dog.

Before I could escape, Caesar turned his head and when he saw me he bounded towards me and when I stepped off the escalator he jumped up in excitement.

The David Jones' girls there were very cross with us, abandoning the dog like we did. One said to me: 'Is this your dog?' I nodded. 'Well, you should be ashamed leaving him like this. He's been very worried!'

Red faced, we left the shopping centre. Personally, I was very annoyed Caesar had 'caused so much trouble,' but my dog didn't care as he had his owner back, he felt safe and his adventure was finally over.

Graeme Frauenfelder

Graeme Frauenfelder is a clown, philosopher, mentor and friend to all. His life stories are inspirational and affirming. He counts his creativity in teams as his greatest accomplishments. Graeme has worked with Patch Adams in the Amazon and is up for any adventure that helps others. Graeme approaches life with sensitivity and dedication.

Send in the Clown

I didn't understand one word of the rapid-fire instructions from the two men at first, but there was no mistaking their intent. There is no ambiguity about a gun waved in your face. My companion and I were compelled to empty our pockets, handing over cameras, wallets and anything else we had.

'This is it,' I thought. My next thought was to wonder if the gun was a fake. Then the men's anger escalated as they screamed, 'Mobile phone! Mobile phone! We kill you! We kill you.'

I didn't have my mobile phone, but I was not believed. They took everything I had with me but that still wasn't enough. The men turned violent. During the attack that followed my thoughts were surreal. I felt a sense of completion about my life. A lack of regret. Then my mind flew to the memory of my 18 year old nephew's death ten weeks earlier and my heart constricted. Another tragedy would be too much for my family. *'I might be ready but they can't take any more'* I worried.

It was December 2008 and I was in Johannesburg with an international group of Fusion volunteers. We were there preparing for community building projects that were associated with World Cup Soccer festivities.

The morning began innocently. The glorious sunrise held no omen of the day ahead. Early in the day, accompanied by our liaison officer Ann, I had the marvellous experience of interacting with African animals, including playing with lion cubs. In one poignant moment, while having a photo taken on the raised platform among the animals, a giraffe rested its head on my shoulder. They were precious photo memories - lost forever on the camera that was later stolen.

After this wonderful time interacting with the animals I expressed to Ann that I would experience an authentic African worship service. Ann took me to a place where colourful groups in traditional clothing met under trees where they sang, danced, chanted and drummed. We had just been blissing out an amazing cultural and spiritual experience observing one of the groups when we were set upon by the two young men.

After negotiating the arduous process of filing a police report for the assault and theft, with Ann using her considerable influence to get them to even do that, I went back to our group quarters. The experience had certainly traumatised me. There were many times when I flinched at shadows, and looked over my shoulder.

However, I continued with the team in creating community festivals in one of the townships and also in another location that brought people of a variety of cultures, religions and socio-economic backgrounds together in a way that they said rarely happened.

My host, Ann, became part of a community initiative that resulted in the two men being caught several months later – after they had mugged over 50 people using a pump action shotgun and usually stabbed their victims. They have just been tried and sentenced to 35 and 45 years in jail. I'm relieved for the people protected from these violent men, but deeply saddened by what led these guys to the crimes, and the waste of their lives.

I often was surrounded by happy, free-spirited children who befriended, helped and played with us. The thought often came to my mind that the two men who had attacked us were once just like these small children. I felt a profound sadness how their lives had turned out and that they had become desperate criminals. It also gave me reassurance that the playful activities, social interaction and community-building projects we were engaged in were worthwhile.

Our reasons for being there were of value, we could be part of influencing the future direction of children's lives. It doesn't get any better than that for me.

It was the most extreme day of my life. Playing with lion cubs, hugging giraffes and going on safari in the morning – then facing death in the afternoon so soon after blissing out in an amazing African cultural and spiritual experience.

My sense of safety, even in my home country is still affected. Part of me is still hyper-alert and wary at times, but I'm glad to be alive. I have no regrets for going to Johannesburg. It was wonderful to be a part of creating meaningful, fun and healing events and activities for many people, across their community and the township. I'll be back one day!

More careful, more alert, but still doing my bit to add sparkle, playfulness and kindness. The richness of many of my experiences in the communities and in nature a couple of summers ago is always in my heart.

John McBride

> **John McBride** claims he swam the Murray River from length to length. He taught Julia Gillard how to box, and he climbed Ayres Rock with his bare teeth. Don't listen to anything he says; read his stories—they bite.

Kitchen table, heart of the Aussie home

It was at the kitchen table that mum sat - day in day out. She made the pastry on it for the pies and tarts. She flattened dough with a milk bottle instead of a rolling pin. She mixed the cakes on it. She sewed our clothes there, altering our school uniforms. As one of my jobs I had to get the bean slicer out of the cupboard, set it up with the screw mechanism on the edge of the table, and slice the beans.

When we came home after school, mum would be at the kitchen table. We would prepare our slice of bread with vegemite and our glass of milk and Quik and sit at the kitchen table and eat and drink.

In the mornings, we would get up, wash, dress and head down to meet as a family at the kitchen table. We would sit there for brekkie, glancing at the front page of the Sun that always had a large picture of news or fashion. I remember at the kitchen table looking at the picture of Jean Shrimpton in her miniskirt at the Cup, the bushfire tragedies, a soaring big-men-fly mark from the weekend football.

At teatime, we sat as a family at the kitchen table. I had a lot of brothers and sisters, so it was quite a gathering every evening. Occasionally the front door bell would ring in the middle of the meal. We kids never did like that. Mum would collect all our plates into the middle before answering the door. If whoever called was asked to stay, the food was reallocated from the collected plates, so there was enough for the unexpected extra eater.

After tea we would sit at the kitchen table and say the Rosary, before we were sent off to sweep floors, take out the rubbish and do our homework.

On Saturdays I would cook. Dad and I both worked in Smith St. He, on the Fitzroy side at Maples furniture shop, and I was on the Collingwood side at EzyWalkins shoe shop. After work, which in those days was soon after midday, I would walk across to Maples and he would drive us home. Once home, I got out the electric frying pan, mixed the hamburgers, added the egg, and the bacon. Then I would stand there as happy as Larry cooking away while siblings came and went, sitting in turns at the table, while I served them their burgers and eggs. Most Saturdays the Parish Priest would call in, 'Not realising it was meal-time'. We always asked him to stay. I don't remember his name: mum and dad referred to him as the Irish Priest. He always added to the atmosphere of Saturday midday with his strong Irish voice, or brogue…it was so strong that everything he said sounded hilarious.

In the later years, when she grew old, mum would sit at the kitchen table most of the day, listening to talk-back radio on 3AW and reading the Women's Weekly. In the evening she would move into the TV room for a while, but would then gravitate back to the kitchen table for her glass of sherry.

Our kitchen table wasn't much to look at. It had a Laminex top, a shiny silver-appearance rim around the edge, and legs that stuck out at strange angles so they got in the way of anyone who wanted to walk past. I actually don't remember what happened to that original table…tables have evolved and become more modern. Somewhere along the line, someone in the family must have had a look at the kitchen table, decided it was old fashioned, ordered a new one, and chucked it out.

My fondest kitchen-table memories are of Sunday lunch. When we were little, we would usually have guests: cousins, uncles and aunts around to Sunday lunch. We were all dressed in our Sunday-best after going to church. After church, while we waited for people to arrive, we stood out in the front yard, all dressed up, talking to neighbours who went past, and then to the various cousins. The lunch was always something grand: no cheap meat like rabbit or stew – no, we had roast lamb or beef, with dobs of gravy and mashed potato, and in the later years, champagne. The adults told stories and we all laughed.

When you think back of happy childhood memories, Sunday lunch was as good as it got.

We all grew up and left home.

Dad died.

Soon we had our own kids.

The years went by without the family meeting on a Sunday.

Whenever a family event happened, though, we still met in that kitchen and sat at that table – major birthdays, wedding anniversaries, kids' birthdays.

When dad died, it was on a Sunday. We all gathered, as did all the relatives: the uncles, the aunts, the cousins-they sat in the kitchen, crammed around the table and over cups of tea, glasses of beer and scones, they talked.

Mum and my brothers and sisters were in the lounge room talking with the priest, and then with the funeral director. The funeral director was a bit too suave and smooth for our liking. He produced forms to sign and packages to tell us about.

We had to choose a coffin.

The funeral Director had a glossy book full of the range of possible coffins, with pictures and prices.

'Why don't people just choose the cheap one?' Mum asked. 'After all, it's just going to be down in the ground, covered with dirt.'

'Well…it might give a bad impression,' replied the funeral director. 'You have to ask yourself, what would the relatives think?'

'Ah, that's easy,' said Mum, 'they're all out there at the kitchen table.'

Before the funeral director could react, Mum had grabbed the catalogue of coffins and headed out to the kitchen to ask the relatives what they would think if we chose the cheaper wooden coffin.

Gradually the Sunday lunch came back. I had my own kids and family; so did my brother; so did my sister. We began to meet again at Mum's house on Sunday at lunchtime. And so, after all those years, there we were again, around that same kitchen table.

Then after a while, the bad times began. My mum's sister was diagnosed with cancer: she and the other sister moved in with mum. Mum herself was getting old and had several falls. The first sister died after a very sad year, and almost immediately the second of mum's sisters was diagnosed with cancer; and the whole cycle started again.

These times were bad; but through it all, we met on Sunday at the kitchen table for lunch. There were old people with dementia and with cancer; but we still drank champagne, and had roast lamb or lunch, and the adults told stories. Though now, *we* were the adults.

And for a while there, every Sunday, as we sat around that table, all the bad things happening in our family had gone away.

After another painful year, the second aunt died. Then mum died only a few months after. The family turned on one another through the stress of those times, and among other things we squabbled over possessions: the crystal cabinet, the antique couch that we had in the lounge room. No one wanted the kitchen table though… which is sad when you consider what that table had seen, and what sitting there in the kitchen had meant to us all those years.

And so, the family home was sold at auction one cold, damp Saturday afternoon. It was during a slump in the housing market and we didn't get much for it. After the auction, we headed off to our own homes, to our own kitchens, and to our own kitchen tables. It was a time to take stock and rebuild.

With our second parent having died, we had all grown up now. But, it didn't feel good. At my place, I sat with my wife and children over a cup of tea, at the kitchen table.

I remember the Kokoda Track

I remember when I was very young, seeing the military great-coat hanging on a nail in the room at the back of the house. This room, called the 'wash-room', contained the copper, scrubbing brush, shoe brush and polish, and other knick-knacks. On a nail behind the door, half hidden by what we called the 'old rag bag' hung a khaki great coat, with a single stripe on the arm and an oval-shaped emblem signifying my father's battalion.

I remember at Christmas time, we thought we were the luckiest children alive. Every year we went to two Christmas parties. One was held on a Saturday afternoon. It was organised by my dad's work, and was called the Maples Christmas party. Why we were lucky was that, when our name was called out, we walked up and received a wrapped present from Father Christmas. The other party was always on a Friday evening. It was held at a military barracks, down in Batman Avenue, I think. I remember it being near Olympic Park, as we walked along the edge of Olympic Park to get there. It was the 39th Battalion Christmas Party. It was held in a hall. At one end, just in front of the stage was a flag on a pole- the flag had the same emblem that hung on the great coat.

I remember as a small child hearing the grownups refer in their conversations to The Blackout, and events that happened 'during the blackout'.

I remember around the corner from our house in Northcote, in the adjoining street, McCracken Avenue, there was a sign on a lamp post saying 'This is a War Savings Street'.

I remember at family parties and gatherings the grownups talked about the good times, the hilarious and major things that happened at a time called 'The end of the war'. I remember as a small child, having a romantic notion of this wonderful time called 'the end of the war'.

I remember on Anzac Day, we would sometimes visit other people's houses. Some years the people we visited had Television, and on Anzac Day it would show documentaries about the war. The film footage always seemed to show ships at sea and aircraft taking off.

I remember when I was ten, getting angry at my mother and calling her a name. I don't remember what the name was; but all of a sudden I felt a blow and went sprawling across the room. I looked up in pain and my father was standing there, red in the face and shaking.

I remember occasionally we would be at someone's house and could hear adults talk. A man would nod in my father's direction and say, 'That's Jack. He was in the 39th Battalion'.

I remember my Uncle John called around one evening with a book by an author named Raymond Paul, titled 'Retreat from Kokoda'. My mum and Uncle John were quite excited; but Dad ignored it all and kept on playing Euchre with Grandpa. Next morning when I got up, the book was still on the kitchen table.

I remember taking the book and speed reading through every page. On page 42, it said , 'At Awala, three days later. Collyer reported to Templeton, proceeding with Pte John McBride from Kokoda to Buna. They returned to Awala on 21st July. As they rested there from the heat, they heard but disregarded a distant rumbling noise which seemed to emanate from the massive banks of clouds, the seat of tropical thunder, in the direction of the coast'.

I remember sitting there in the kitchen and thinking about my dad, resting in the jungle hearing sounds like thunder in the distance. I remember the magic and the romance and the pride, as I sat there a small boy, at the kitchen table in Northcote.

I remember when a teenager, occasionally there would be a story in the Sun newspaper about the Kokoda Track. My mother would cut it out and paste it in an exercise book.

I remember as a teenager watching the Anzac Day parade on television, and getting a thrill when they described the 'heroes' of the 39th Battalion as they proudly marched past. I also remember that Dad never showed any interest in going to the Anzac Day parade.

I remember, one day when the family was together around a picnic table, I told a story. 'One day a boy dropped his watch over the side of a boat when at sea. Years later, he was at the kitchen table preparing a fish to cook for tea and the knife he was holding cut into something hard - it was his thumb.' I heard a sound, looked up and saw my father laughing.

I remember as an adult, many years later when my father died that was the only time I had ever seen him laugh.

I remember as I grew older, the references to the Kokoda Track became more and more frequent at family gatherings, and there were more and more occasions where people pointed out my father to neighbours and cousins and told about the 39th Battalion.

I remember none of those conversations ever included Dad. He was in the distance, and was whispered about.

I remember when I was about thirty years old; I visited my parents one evening with my wife and young family. I was about to go to Japan for a scientific conference. My father acted very uneasy, and said he did not like me going to Japan. I tried to question him; but he would not talk.

I remember the day my father died. My wife, children and I were visiting my parents for Sunday lunch. On the way across the suburbs we stopped at the Camberwell market; so we arrived at lunch a little late. When we arrived, there were several cars around my parents' house. My brother Adrian answered the door. I asked what he was doing there, and he told me 'Dad died this morning.'

I remember about fifteen years later, Mum died. Society had changed then such that at funerals it had become common for a member of the family to give a eulogy during the funeral. I sat up during the night working hard, using all the professional skills acquired over the years in my profession, trying to write a eulogy that did justice to my mother.

The eulogy was a description of my mother's life; and my delivery took 20 to 30 minutes. Near the start I mentioned that she met my father before the beginning of the war; that at Christmas time 1941 he left for New Guinea; he was a member of a famous Battalion that was massacred and reformed several times; and that he spent the entire war on the frontline in New Guinea, at one stage having been declared 'missing in action', and that he travelled home in 1945 to marry my mother. Throughout my childhood their black and white wedding photo stood proudly in a frame on their bedroom dresser, with Dad in his military uniform. In the eulogy I mentioned he was always ill after the war, but that he struggled to work at the furniture shop in Smith St Fitzroy, until finally in the seventies he was declared Totally and Permanently Incapacitated (TPI) resulting from his war service; and was pensioned off until his death in 1981. This was a very small part of my mother's eulogy taking a few minutes.

I remember after the funeral, standing in the foyer of the church while friends and well-wishers came up and grasped me and comforted me. My cousin Lester said the words about my father and the war meant a lot to him: 'That bloody war,' he said. 'I grew up with a father sitting inside and not talking to us'. Then another male friend stopped by and told essentially the same story; then another… so I was standing there in an emotional state thinking we were an entire generation who grew up with fathers who were physically present, but whose minds were far away.

I remember visiting my father's grave many years later, with my second wife, who had not been there during my middle age, during my father's death, and my mother's death. We drove to the Preston cemetery and walked through the aisles of graves, and came across a soldier's grave, low-lying and unadorned, with my name on it: 'Sergeant John McBride'. And in gold engraving was that same symbol of the rising sun that I saw on the great coat and in the sewing machine drawers all those years before. I remember not being able to speak, my voice choking, with my new and younger wife wondering why I cried so long and so hard simply when visiting a cemetery.

I remember only a few months ago walking through a bookshop in town with my 19 year old daughter (who lives with her mother). On the display-stand at the front of the shop was a display of a book titled 'Kokoda' with a cover photo of Australian soldiers from my father's era. I said to my daughter, 'I suppose you know your grandfather, my dad, was at Kokoda'. My daughter said, 'No, I didn't know that. I have heard about Kokoda at school many times. I didn't know there was any personal connection'.

I remember buying a book in the Johannesburg Airport, about growing up in South Africa. The style was interesting and unique. The book was titled 'We walk straight so you better get out of the way' by Denis Hirson. Every paragraph of the book began with the phrase 'I remember….' Reading Hirso's book on the plane on my way home from South Africa. As I sat there in Business Class, relaxing and sipping a glass of wine, I had the idea to write this story.

I remember being a 55 year old man, sitting in Business Class on my recliner seat, sipping a glass of wine, with tears rolling down my face … the pain of Kokoda has not finished yet.

Two tone shoes

In the fifties, when I was a kid growing up in Northcote, there were two 'tribes'. It was we 'Australians' with surnames like 'McBride' and 'Doyle' and 'Moloney'; and there were the 'Italians' with surnames like 'Gaetano', 'Munzone' and 'Benedetti'. The Italians and the Australians lived side by side in tidy rows of weatherboard houses with corrugated iron roofs and picket fences. Though gradually the 'Italians' turned their weatherboard houses into brick veneer by simply covering the boards with a wall of orange brick. My mum got on marvellously with the other tribe. She liked to stop and chat. She loved the new types of cheese you could get by calling in on them in the afternoons; she loved their parties in the backyard on weekends with music, laughter and drink. And she loved the exotic drinks they would serve up to her in little ornate glasses: the Crème de Menthe and the Marsala.

Mum never figured out any of their surnames. She would say to me: 'John, Nick down to the Italians around the corner and see if they want any of these biscuits I just made,' or 'Nick down to the Italians down the street and borrow a cup of flour'. We coexisted, and gradually we blended. Back in Northcote at St Joseph's Primary School there were many more of 'them' than there were of 'us'. Looking at the Grade Three school photo I have in a cupboard, there are about ten of we Doyles, McBrides and Moloneys, compared to about sixty Gaetanos and Benedettis. The two tribes travelled together along High St and Smith St on the tram on the way to school. We visited one another's houses on the way home from school. We played with one another in the yard and in the street; and we went to the footy together at the MCG on Saturday afternoons. I knew we were different, but it wasn't until I was much older, maybe thirty or forty years down the track before I learned what the difference was. The difference, dear reader, was that they were more fashionable than us.

I am an Anglo-Saxon Australian, third generation. My great grandfather on Dad's side came over from Ireland at the end of the 19th century. Mum's grandparents came from England around the same time. I am also a public servant, and also a scientist. So, I am pretty nerdy, pretty conservative, pretty Anglo-Australian. I grew up wearing Fletcher Jones trousers, and Glo-weave shirts, with Brylcream on my hair. As I grew older, and became an adult, and went to work I remained unfashionable. I wore a jumper to work, with a narrow tie and I carried a brown leather brief case, with a worn handle.

My second wife, on the other hand, who I married forty years later is Italian…and…she's very fashionable. Being a good Australian man I owned two pair of shoes that I would wear to work in my office in the city. I owned a brown pair that I would wear with certain sets of clothes, and a black pair that matched all my other clothes.

One day, I was walking along the street and the sole came loose on the black pair…so, out in Collins St at lunchtime, suddenly I was walking along like Bozo the clown, with my shoe making a flop, flop, flop sound as I walked. There are two courses of action open when your shoe reaches the end of its useful life. The first is that you can get on the tram, travel up to Myers, and buy a replacement pair of shoes…sensible Australian shoes, made of leather, with laces, and so on. Or… you can go home that evening and mention to your fashionable Italian wife that you need a new pair of shoes. I did the latter.

So the following weekend my fashionable Italian wife organises me so that we get in the car and drive out to Coburg to the shoe factories and outlet stores. I walk in to one of these outlet shoe places…there are shoes displayed in boxes all around the perimeter of the factory wall…I see a nice conservative looking replacement pair…lace-up, leather…the sort I've worn all my life.

I take the shoe off the box and am trying it on. Then I look up and see my wife and the factory owner…an elder, very fashionable-looking Italian gent looking at me, shaking their heads. The next thing I know I am handed a pair of two-tone shoes…the left side of the shoe is white…the right side is black. The shoe is made of leather, with laces; but it has the lines and the style of a running shoe.

I panic. I look around for help…there is no help…my wife and the factory owner are insistent…I try the shoes on…we buy them.

Next Monday I'm in at work…walking the corridors, attending the seminar, having scientific discussions, joining my friends for morning tea…all in two-tone Italian shoes. They laugh. They snigger. At the beginning of the seminar, after presenting the highly mathematical title of the talk, the speaker breaks the ice and engages the audience by making a joke about two-tone shoes.

The following week I was due to fly up to Brisbane to attend a special Conference on the topic of Australian Storms, organised jointly by the Meteorological Societies of Australia and New Zealand. I was speaking with my boss, the famous scientist Neville Nicholls before I left:

'You're not going to wear those shoes to Brisbane?' he asked jokingly in disbelief.

I went home to pack for the conference. My fashionable Italian wife insisted I wear the two-tone shoes. I was giving two presentations at the Storms Conference – One on tropical cyclones and one on what is likely to happen to major rainfall events under global warming. The first day of the conference seemed to go well. Though at the opening ice-breaker and at the morning tea breaks, there seemed to be a lot of discussion about shoes. I called my wife from the hotel that evening.

'There are about two hundred scientists up here in Brisbane', I said. 'One hundred and ninety nine of them seem to be joking about my shoes.

Being an older scientist, I get a bit of a kick out of engaging the younger scientists and the students at tea breaks and lunch sessions at these meetings. On the following day, I was talking to an attractive young female scientist, probably in her thirties as we helped ourselves to scones while we juggled our saucer and tea cup. 'I like your shoes', she said. I tried to steer the conversation to tropical cyclone dynamics.

Later that day, I went with a group for lunch in a local sandwich bar. This group also included a number of younger female scientists and PhD students. I was sitting with one of them while we ate and chatted about careers and about Brisbane. She paused mid-conversation, and said, 'By the way, I love those shoes. They really suit you.'

That afternoon, I gave the first of my two conference presentations, the one on tropical cyclones. I always feel drained after the experience of putting together a major presentation like that; so I left the conference early that day, and walked by myself back towards the hotel.

On the way, I stopped at another little sandwich bar to have a coffee and to relax. As I was sitting there at an outside table, I heard the voice of a young waitress as she approached: 'Hey…what a great pair of shoes!'

This is John, in his fifties, scientist, nerd, has been unfashionable all his life. I phoned my wife again from the hotel:

'I've changed my mind', I said, 'I like these shoes.'

And I flew back to Melbourne and to work the following week, and I wore those two-tone shoes every day to work in the city and to the various scientific conferences I attended around the nation. I wore them until the soles were worn down. Eventually one Sunday evening, they were finished, and I carried them out to the street and placed them in the rubbish bin out there on the nature strip.

And that is the story of the two-tone shoes.

James Ward

James Ward is an accomplished poet and novelist. James Ward is a specialist English as Second Language teacher who has worked with remote area Aboriginal students. James has taught in Arnhem Land, the Kimberleys and the Central Australian Desert.

The Blackfella Wisdom of Albert

Old Albert Bailey was a wise old black man. He was into his seventies when I knew him. He had a calm, deeply furrowed boot-polish-black face overlaid with the softness of red pindan sand dust and a shy kindliness. He was the Law man for all the Dreamings of the Sandover area and lived at a tiny lost Aboriginal community called Entarraninya, about seventy dusty, blood red kilometres from Utopia, north east of Alice Springs. He was an Umutjarra man. A fully initiated man, wise and calm far beyond that wisdom and calmness to be found in the aged 'whitefellas' of our time. I often used to sit in the 45 degree heat and dust with Albert and his scabies riddled dogs and let the serenity around him sink into my troubled hyperactive white man' soul.

You know Pwerla, he said one day, They used to shoot at us mob ... back when I was a boy ... we had to hide in the bush all day and sneak out to the soaks to get water at night ... anybody ... them whitefellas all tried to kills us mob...' But he bore no malice just the ancient patience of the black man. I remember asking him if his tribe fought with the tribe next door in the old days. Before the white man came. He thought long and hard, obviously puzzled by the question. Then he looked at me as if I was a fool and asked me, 'Why would we fight with them?...they were our neighbours!' Anyway I got to love old Albert and his shy younger wife and looked forward to the few days every week I spent in their tiny extremely isolated desert community with its surrounding low hills and wild Spinifex and desert oaks.

There was a younger Walpri man living there 'married' to one of the local ladies and Albert found it a chore to tolerate this strong and cheeky younger fella. I could tell. Even though his ancient manners meant I never heard him speak a word against him. The young Walpri man was called Keith. He was a student of mine learning English.

Some weeks earlier Keith's wife, a good artist, had left him, and taken their two children to Umbluderwhich (spelt phonetically as I can't use the accepted orthography!!!), a desert community about 120 kms north east of Utopia. On my return to Alice Keith asked could he get a lift to town. It was 340 kms and difficult for desert Aboriginals to visit from such a small out-of-the-way community. I said he could and got a sob story about the loss of his wife and 'shildren' all the way to Alice. He sang sad songs in his language loving them and showed me several lovely pictures of these kids. He told me his mother-in-law had lured his wife away from him. She was a drunk. He reckoned she wanted access to his wife's money from painting and that she was a wicked woman. On the way to town I asked Keith if he'd been drinking. 'No!' was the firm reply. Followed by, '... Maybe little bit been drin 'im...' Following a long pause I asked, 'Keith, you been hit this woman?'

Once again, outraged 'No!' Followed a few seconds later with 'Well maybe little bit bin kill in...' (Hit her). (Kill'im proper means 'kill.')

Oh I thought, so the true story is emerging.

I got to town and spent over an hour trying yet again to sort out one of the incredibly complex messes that semi traditional aboriginals get into trying to interface with whitefella culture. Some idiot had given Keith a credit card! With a limit of $1500!!!! He was now well over the limit and some Mercantile Collection agency in Melbourne was trying to collect the money—fat chance. I laughed as I imagined the Melbourne based clerk trying to envisage what or where was Enterreninya! The bank teller got the shits and kept pumping on the button to release a refreshing odour around her as Keith, and possibly my good self, after a week in the desert had a certain hummmm.

Finally it was all too hard. Keith had lost his bankcard and lost his pin number and couldn't get a new one as the address was the address his wife was staying at and he had an order out on him not to go anywhere near her as it turned out or he would go back to gaol and finish his 18 months for assault on his wife.

My God. The story as it unravelled was like a hundred other stories I had heard since starting to work with this mob of desert blackfellas. I told Keith I would run him to his 'family' before I clocked off for the week and sorted a hot shower in my own humble abode in Alice.

Keith found his family in the sunny afternoon in one of the town's lovely oaks no doubt having a few early after afternoon sherberts and so I dropped him off there with them. The following week before I went out again, I heard from a colleague who taught English at the Alice gaol.

'I have a new student,' he smirked, 'one of your mates.' Apparently, Keith, who was so sad about losing his family, drank himself into a stupor in the park with his mob, then got a lift to his mother-in-laws' where he bit the shit out of her and belted the be-Jesus out of his wife. Hence his return to prison to serve the last fifteen month of his suspended sentence plus six months. I was nervous. I had driven Keith to town and I might be in for payback from old Albert and his mob. I had already tangled with the Aboriginal culture around issues such as 'payback' several times and didn't ever want to again.

I arrived there on the Wednesday to teach for the rest of the week. And went immediately to see old Albert to see how the land lay. I apologised profusely for my unintentional part in the saga. And asked old Albert if I was in any trouble for driving Keith to Alice. Eventually after considering the far off hills and the distant clouds with his trachoma damaged old eyes he answered me, just above a whisper.

'...Sometimes Pwerla... it's better to do nothing...'

Feeling relieved that there was to be no consequences for what I had thought was a friendly gesture, giving a guy a ride to town I walked off pondering his reply. Yes, I thought you mob have had a lot of time; forty thousand years in fact, to work that out!

Longing For Beaches

My heart is aching
For a breaking wave,
And all the teeming life
Of tiny pools

My heart is longing
For a stretch of white hot sand,
And to walk along it
Hand in hand
On a beach of fools,
Convinced that
The coloured things
They're collecting
From the water's edge
Are pirate's jewels
And mermaid's rings.

From so far away,
I can only dream
Of that endless arc of sky
And the salty shock of spray
Spun off a wall of deep green sea

From so, so far away from that blue
The terns and the gulls
Are calling me
And so are you.

How would my soul forgive me,
If I stayed and died
So far away from the singing waters
And the drumbeat of the tide?

James Ward

Desert

I came to the desert to forget you
To travel here with Kaffka
And to read Albert Camus...
But it is red this country
Its blood spilled on its sandy flesh.

And it reminds me always of the bright blood
between us that once turned our bathwater red
That once printed cryptic roses on our youthful bed.

It is so red this country... it is so red at mungati
Blood covering its evening skies
It is so, so red this country
As red as the blood that once
Long ago, covered your trembling thighs.

So what can I tell you now, Woman that once I loved
More than my own soul... What can I tell you
Of innocence and death You with whom I once
Shared breath...

What can I tell you As the long dream rips
And I can only whisper to you Through broken lips?

Only that out here I have to suffer
The migraines of yellow budgerigars
The arrogant ghosts of the Dreaming...
The gestalt of the screeching galahs
And an obsession to walk all night
Going blind, just picking up stars.

The Old Homestead

I dreamt last night I went to Palmers* once again,
And slept in the old brass bed and heard the river tide
I dreamt last night that I lay again with my dark haired bride
And my children were young and innocent again with shining eyes
I dreamt they were completely happy, just playing at our side…
Children of the surf and sand and sun, with voices like seagulls' cries.

I dreamt there was a black yacht on the river
Waiting for me, tied up to a darkling buoy,
I dreamt of the sugar ship, sounding its shrill siren like a warning…
But I dreamt the old house laughed and danced again
And all of us were young and Ouzo drunk with joy…
I dreamt that this would last forever and we'd sing and shout
And watch the tropic sun set, every silken night,
And I dreamt we still ate marmalade and mangoes in the morning…

Not knowing that our tide of happiness was already running out.

Last night I dreamed I went to Palmers once again…
And everything was right and Andy's eyes still had their gleam
Last night I dreamed I went to Palmers once again…
And all the terrible years since then, had been a dream.

*Palmers is Palmers Island on the lower Clarence River.

James Ward

I Loved a Young Girl Once

I thought an old love,
Would stay sweet
As fruit straight off the vine
Not tannin-bitter and
Vinegary like mine...

I loved a young girl once,
Her hair and eyes
Gave me no surprise
Nor her breasts
Full bounce...

And I dreamed,
As only a boy can dream
Of growing softly old
With only her to hold
And an old age warm...
But mine is cold...

Ah of love and lips
There is no secret code
Just a sad and lonely road,
Where now you limp

Where once you strode
And an unpleasant bitterness
To the wine one sips
When age becomes
A far too heavy load....

Our Parting

We did not ask for this,
Nor for the camphor laurels
Fare welling evening
With a goodbye kiss…
We didn't ask for the acid
Turning our blood sour,
Or the fading intimacy
Of this grieving hour…
We didn't ask for the fall
Of night in our hearts,
Or the cruel baptism
Of us both crying in the bath
Before sadly walking away,
From a great love's aftermath.

James Ward

The Channon*

After the dance was over
We drove out to Howard's farm
The cattle in the moonlit clover,
You walked in on my arm...
We smoked out last joint
And finished the bourbon
Left in Howard's fridge,
Then while you went to bed
I went outside for an hour
To watch the moonlight on the ridge...
When I finally came to bed
You were fast asleep
Your heart and soul at rest,
Your dark hair on the pillow
The moonlight on your breast,
Tight dark curls covering your cleft...
Now forty years have fled,
But not the jangling guilt,
For I have never forgotten,
You sleeping so sweetly,
Beneath that fine silver quilt
Of The Channon moonlight on our bed.

Watching you in that silent room
That my heart had already left.

*The Channon is a delightful small farming village and community in the rainforest about 25 kms west of Lismore, NSW.

Barrie Ridgway

Barrie Ridgway is a retired bank manager with a fine sense of literary prose and humour. His keen eye for detail and editing skills make him a valuable contributor to this anthology.

My first customer

It was an auspicious day for 'The Wales', they had made a very wise decision to employ me.

So on 15th March 1957 I rode my pushbike down the hill to the bank instead of to school.

Having gained admission to the premises I was introduced to the staff, Mr Clements the Manager, Mr Butler the Accountant, Mr Hope-Hume the teller, Edward (Ted) Schmitt, Vai Males and Kaye Barton. Kaye was to be my mentor so she set about showing me what my duties would be and at what time they were to be carried out. For instance the mail had to be collected from the Post Office box at 9.00 am and all staff had to have their tea and biscuits by 9.30 am.

After that the customer area was to be checked for clean blotters, fresh nibs in pens, full inkwells and a proper supply of deposit and withdrawal slips. At 10.00 am sharp the front door of the bank was to be opened and I was to be first call on the enquiry counter.

Not long after I had opened the doors and greeted a couple of customers who had been waiting I stationed myself behind the enquiry counter, a polished slab of two inch thick jarrah which was some four feet wide and ten feet long. Kaye however called me away to start the process of teaching me how transactions dealt with by the teller had to be recorded. Deposits (credits) on one side; cash and cheques (debits) on the other thus I commenced learning the basics of accountancy.

Out of the corner of my eye I saw a black raffia hat adorned with plastic flowers approaching the enquiry counter. I quickly moved to the counter to see two eyes peering up at me and a concerned voice asking me if she could see the manager on a matter of great urgency.

Having ascertained her name I went over to the door of the manager's office, knocked and waited to be called in.

After I had advised him that Mrs Dear was anxious to see him I was advised to get her a cup of tea, white and two sugars plus two 'Nice' biscuits, while he ushered her into his office. We had some quality bone china for customers use so there were no problems.

After the customer left the manager came out to advise the staff Mrs Dear had lost her chequebook and she was concerned someone may misuse it. Care was to be exercised and all transactions thoroughly perused.

These were the days when there were no account numbers or names printed on personal cheque forms, staff had to recognise customers' signatures or in need, refer to a chequebook register to see who had been issued with that specific chequebook.

Later, while the manager was at lunch, Mrs Dear returned and asked to see him.

On being told the manager wasn't available she asked me to tell him not to worry about the unused forms in the chequebook. They were no good to anyone else because she had signed them all.

The 'black' kangaroo

I was three years old at the time of this story. An age where my own recollections are blurred with the stories told to me by two older cousins, Joan and Patricia, their grandparents' account and photographs. Who knows where one starts and the other ends? Recalling what happened was made more difficult by the fact that I'd been sent to relatives at Margaret River, in rural West Australia during the war, to be 'out of harm's way'.

Years later, I was lucky enough to be transferred to Margaret River for a time by my employer. I was able to visit the property. This helped me find perspective on my time there.

In 1942 Japanese military expansion across the southern Pacific towards Australia seemed to be unstoppable. With my father, a RAN officer serving in the Pacific, and my mother engaged in 'war work' in Perth, Joan, Patricia and I were sent to the relative safety of Margaret River. This was seen as an unlikely military target. Joan was about thirteen and Patricia was about eleven. Their father was serving in the RAAF. The cousins' grandparents took us into their home.

They organised schooling for the girls. I was apparently allowed to pursue the usual things which attracted preschool boys of the time.

One of those activities was 'helping' grandpa and grandma Bremner in the vegie garden. Grandpa Bremner was a PMG technician who had been manpowered to ensure the telephone system remained viable. Growing vegies and sending them off was also seen as a valuable contribution to the war effort.

The kangaroos resident in the adjacent State forest were a problem. They also had a great liking for fresh veggies. A stout fence of considerable height managed to protect most of the garden, but some of the more determined roos broke through.

During one of these forays a joey was left behind and grandma Bremner raised it. By the time I and my fellow 'evacuees' arrived the joey was quite a size, but very much at home with humans. It assessed me as no threat, so I was able to hug it and generally treat it as a large, warm, furry friend.

Early one morning I found a tin of lovely black stuff. It was shoe polish, and in no time at all both the kangaroo and I took on a blotchy black complexion. I cannot recall what prompted me, or how I set about it, but I had changed the appearance of my furry friend and myself considerably. I guess I was just 'doing what boys do'. While grandma Bremner and cousin Pat scrubbed me clean, Joan got the 'rough' off the kangaroo, tidied up and headed off to school. Once I was no longer looking like a chimney sweep Pat was left with the chore of cleaning herself up. She was very late for school and copped a stern rebuke from her teacher for telling such a 'tall tale'. Imagine the teacher's surprise when she checked with grandma Bremner and found the whole saga was true. She apologised profusely. Everyone had a good laugh and a story to tell.

Like all boys, I found the cleaning process and the female fussing that went with it so distasteful, that I never repeated this trick. Although I'm sure I found other 'activities' that kept my temporary family on their toes.

Mrs Pierson's frequent visits

Back in the days when farmers had acres and lived miles from town journeys along rough, dusty gravel roads, or in winter, wet slushy, slippery roads could easily make trips to town an inconvenient task. When coupled with the existence of inferior public toilets, it meant that 'visits' were only made on a needs basis. This experience was far from pleasant and nothing the poor country folk tried to do seemed to improve the arrangement.

However, being away from their own homes meant things like clean toilets, aka dunnies, outhouses, thunderboxes, loos or lavs, were always sought out and filed in the memory bank in case of need. The country folk were keen to take advantage of salubrious surroundings for this all important task.

Our family lived in town, thus we possessed a prime 'dunny'. Mind you, we never heard our cultured mother refer to the outhouse arrangement in those terms. She refused to use the word.

One hot summer day my younger brother, Trevor and I were wiling away the hours as young boys do when we overheard a remark made by our mother to a friend. We were young and restless – I was ten and Trevor was seven at the time. Bored by the lack of the usual entertainments we took keen notice of the conversation.

'I swear that woman only visits here to use our toilet. She always asks if Norm (dad) has checked it for redbacks, if the phenyle has been used to moderate the pong and if there is an adequate supply of toilet paper then heads off to use the facility,' said mother.

The toilet involved was a pan system type with a big flap at the back so the 'dunny man' could remove the used pan and replace it with a fresh one every week. The dunny man, as all the kids knew, not only came at night to carry out his job, he also drove the most powerful truck in town, it had 96 'piss tins'.

Our mother was very houseproud and paid great attention to our dunny. The seat, with appropriate hole, was made of a smooth plank of Jarrah. There was a row of 'accessories' to enhance the experience, or more likely the cleanliness and odour.

Apples in those days were purchased in large boxes and wrapped individually in soft green tissue-paper squares. These tissues were there for the purpose of wiping down backsides and, along with a good splash of Methylated Spirits and, the seat after use. Having to keep this high standard was a chore for young boys, but in spite of our grumblings we were grateful for mother's care. Her statement stuck in our minds. Anyway, not long after our flapping ears had overheard this remark, the lady in question called for a visit, had a chat and cuppa then asked the usual question, 'Do you mind if I…'

Having received the usual assurances she headed off to the toilet. My brother had anticipated this and, equipped with a long piece of splintered bamboo, stationed himself behind the dunny. Once things settled down inside he quietly lifted the flap and probed with the bamboo.

A scream split the air. The door which usually opened inward, burst outward, causing considerable strain on the hinges. As we peeked around, we saw a large rotund figure bolting across the yard towards the gate. Mrs Pierson was clutching her left derriere, with her ample drawers hanging significantly below her 'town dress'.

She never did make a return visit, and mother's attempts to give my brother and me a 'good ticking off' were hampered by her inability to keep a straight face.

Wartime fishing trip

My father rarely spoke of the more unpleasant aspects of war, either as experienced by him or by his contemporaries; however; he was happy to relate stories about the more humorous incidents if the mood was right.

With the glorified title of 'Victualling Officer, Allied Navies, South West Pacific Area' my father, a RANVR Lt Commander, was on Thursday Island in August 1942 at a time when things were starting to go in favour of the Allies. The Axis powers (Germans, Italians and Vichy French) were running out of steam in North Africa and the Russians were taking their toll as they defended their homeland.

In PNG the Japanese had successfully landed at Buna and Gona and were trying to push on over the Owen Stanley Range to Port Moresby. This was a last ditch effort by the Japs as the Coral Sea battle in early May and Battle of Midway In early June had sapped their naval strength ruling out a seaborne assault on Port Moresby. Also in the South West Pacific ongoing clashes in the Solomon Islands saw massive losses on both sides, one casualty being HMAS Canberra during a night engagement on 8/9th August.

In anticipation of a Japanese assault Australian forces had established a strategically located base at Milne Bay, situated on the south-east tip of New Guinea. All arms of the Australian forces were represented, Navy, Army and Airforce. The move to Milne Bay to assist in co-ordinating the flow of supplies to all who were involved was quite a challenge. Aside from foodstuff, ammunition, fuel, medical supplies etc being landed, stored and distributed there were other tasks being performed. A Communication centre, Signal Station, field hospital and an airstrip had to be constructed.

Next to the Japanese the most dangerous foes were the malarial mosquitoes. From there, Dad, when he eventually arrived home, brought some foul tasting quinine tablets which cured my younger brother of his thumb sucking habit.

On August 25th the Japs landed well equipped troops on the northern side of Milne Bay and fierce fighting by Australian and American soldiers forced the Japs to evacuate the survivors on August 29th.

In the face of strong defence by Australian soldiers and, in part because the Allies controlled the air and destroyed their supply lines, the Japanese assault across the Owen Stanley Range petered out Ioribawa Ridge, about 48 kilometres from Port Moresby.

This was the 'turning of the tide' and the Japanese were pushed back to their landing points at Buna and Gona. Along the northern coast of PNG the RAN beach-masters established supply depots where material ranging from tanks and artillery to ammunition and foodstuff were gathered in preparation for a final assault on the trapped Japanese.

One more desperate Japanese attempt to salvage their invasion of PNG resulted in the Battle of the Bismark Sea when, over two days the entire twenty two ship convoy of troopships and their escorts which were headed for Lae, was totally destroyed by RAAF and USAF aircraft.

While the preceding is recorded history available to anyone it is intended to give the reader a perspective of one incident which was related to me by one of my father's fellow officers, Lt Hugh Rudderham RANVR, who served alongside him. Mr Rudderham subsequently resumed his civilian career and retired as General Manager, Fremantle Harbour Trust.

Some time after the Battle of the Bismark Sea when allied airforces controlled the air it was felt a little R & R (rest and relaxation) was overdue, as was a change of diet, so a fishing expedition was organised. The enemy was supposed to be retreating and, aside from some nuisance air raids, wasn't posing much of a local threat.

In the harbour was a Fairmile launch, whether it was an 85 long ton British B Type or a 79 long ton Canadian B Type I don't know but either variation was well armed with one twin and one single 20 mm Oerlikon anti-aircraft gun and probably a couple of twin .303 inch machineguns. The Canadian version handled better but the British one had an armour plated wheelhouse. There were also depth charges and a deck gun as optional extras.

The RAN purchased 35 boats and ended the war with 33. They came in a six pack kit form and I believe they were assembled in Australia by Green Point Boatyard; Halvorsen and Norman Wright.

Early one morning a volunteer crew mustered onboard and off they went to catch some fish and generally relax. After some time at sea two Japanese aircraft flew over and took an interest in the boat, they dropped to strafing level and lined up the boat.

The Oerlikon gunners responded and 'splashed' both aircraft. Apparently the aircraft were purely reconnaissance types and the Japanese were running out of more experienced pilots.

When they fished out a surviving pilot; he roundly abused them in perfect 'Oxford English'. It transpired he had been educated in England.

Graeme Brown

Graeme Brown is a second generation Australian with a crisp memory of the family's struggles and his early life in rural Australia. For the Brown's improvisation was a way of life, one that has been the bedrock of his adult years.

Dad's Orchard

My grandfather came to the Antipodes from Great Britain in 1915 and started an orchard. Dad eventually took it over. We grew apricots, pears, peaches and plums, and had a few apple trees and four lemon trees. We had no electricity, using only manpower and horsepower.

The house seemed as if it had never been completed. The wall between what we called The Porch and the garage was made of hessian, and the weatherboard walls had never been painted. To accommodate us children Dad built a sleepout under the verandah, constructed largely from hessian, and for a while I slept in a tent in the front yard.

The bathroom contained only the bathtub with a large crack in it, filled by a four gallon drum of water heated on the kitchen stove. Later we got a bath heater, fired by kindling. The rooms were lined with horizontal wooden boards, except the parlour, which was papered over the boards. The room which we called the porch, which had a cement floor, contained the ice chest, coolgardie safe and meat safe. On a wall in a corner was the telephone, which looked like a face - the two bells for eyes, mouthpiece for nose, a ledge for a mouth, and the earpiece hook in place of an ear. One of the chimneys had a distinct lean and was pulling away from the house—we were scared that one day it would fall.

The sheds, next to the horse paddock, were a far cry from the typical Men's Shed of today. There was the chaff house, stocking the horse feed, and shelters for the lorry, spray pump, plough and cultivator. Later this space was modified to provide rudimentary accommodation for pickers. The harnesses, curry comb etc. hung on walls, while the shovels, pick, mattock and crowbar stood against the walls. Granny's chook house was a little further away.

Washing was done by means of the copper in the back yard, heated by kindling. After boiling in water with Velvet soap, the clothes were blued, put through the mangle, and hung on the clothes line - a wire strung around the yard and held up by wooden props. The rainwater tank stood against the bathroom wall. When mosquitoes started breeding in the water Dad would pour in half a cup of kerosene – into the drinking water. There was only enough rain water for drinking - water for washing was pumped from the irrigation channel by windmill. At a respectable distance from the house was the typical country-style toilet, and a child's swing swung from a nearby tree branch.

Lighting was by kerosene table lamps, and a hurricane lantern for outside use. The plough, cultivator and spray pump were, of course, horse drawn. The spray pump presented a problem, as the noisy 2-stoke motor scared the horse. The pump was used to spray DDT, Arsenate of Lead and other chemicals as the fruit was growing - at that time no-one was aware of the dangers of such substances. Grandpa still had his gig, drawn by one horse, which he and Granny used occasionally, but we also had a car.

We only used the grey 1926 Morris Cowley Tourer for our Saturday morning trip into 'Town'. Starting it was quite a procedure. Dad would heat water in a four gallon drum on the stove, pour it into the radiator, and give a few turns of the crank handle. If this did not work he would hitch up one of the horses to tow the car to jump start it. When we eventually arrived in town it was a rush to get round the grocers, butchers, bakers, greengrocers, ironmongers, etc. before they closed at noon. A three penny ice cream cone was a real treat for us children. Last was the dairy - we wanted to get the block of ice last so it would not melt so much. When we ran out of bread (six pence for a full loaf, or three pence for a half loaf) Mum made oatcakes for the rest of the week. Usually a neighbouring orchardist had a cow, so we never ran out of milk. It became my job to ride across for the six penny quart in the billycan before school.

Irrigation made the whole venture possible. Water from the main channel behind the orchard went through a narrow channel, under a water wheel which measured it, into smaller channels which distributed it round the orchard, and then into furrows beside the rows of trees, all controlled by shovel.

The busiest time, of course, was picking. Fruit was picked into bags, then emptied into wooden boxes and taken to the grading table. Here each piece was inspected and graded for size by passing through metal rings, and the boxes of fruit were taken either to the markets or the cannery for canning or jam.

Dad had to sell the orchard in 1950, after a run of bad seasons. I saw the property many years later. The present owners have built a brick house where the apricot trees had been, and the old house is used seasonally by pickers. The chimney is still standing, and the place still needs a good coat of paint. The sheds have all gone, and in their place is a massive storage facility for the fruit. And they now have a tractor, and electricity!

Martin Killips

Martin Killips is a renowned poet and artist. His work is full of whimsy and delight. He regularly visits schools and spreads the joy of creativity with children and other writers. Visit Martin at
http://www.thebigbamboo.com.au

Lost For Words!
(A warning to all slovenly bachelors)

There was a man who grew quite fat
and though he kept himself a cat,
he hadn't caught himself a wife
so lived a rather lonely life.

Now when a man lives on his own,
albeit with a cat at home,
he's very prone to misbehave -
in keeping with all untrained knaves.
Their habits slip, their routines slide,
(drink straight from bottles - I'll confide);
Leave loo seats up when they are finished -
their social skills are much diminished.

Now our man - who we'll call Tubby,
(who had no wife - and was no hubby)
would eat baked-beans straight from the can
then lick the lid - the stupid man;
For even children know that's dumb -
cos licking tin lids cuts your tongue!
And porcine Tubby, at the trough,
licked so damn hard he sliced his off!

OUCH!

Imagine that! He sliced it off!
Had no tongue left to shout or scoff!
And on the floor the tongue lay still,
or rather did at first, until
he went to grab it so some quack
could try their best to sew it back;
But as he reached, the tongue went flip!

Then flop! Then slop! Then slap! Then slip!
Then demonstrating extra zoom,
it somersaulted out the room!

The man just panicked: tried to shout -
But with no tongue no words came out!
Just sounds like 'Wee' and 'Woo' and 'Waugh'
So nothing said made sense at all!

His flapping tongue just flipped away -
(the slug-like trail behind it stayed!)
And cos the backdoor was ajar
tongue headed for the nearest bar!

But sitting on the backdoor mat
was Tubby's hungry pussy cat;
And nothing brings a cat to pounce
than something flipped with extra bounce!

One snarl! One leap! One growl! One bite!
And Tubby's tongue soon lost the fight;
The pussy cat just licked its lips
and mused: 'That tongue needs extra chips!'

Poor Tubby's tongue was not replaced:
if spoken to he'd leave in haste;
And after *silent* Tubbs had gone
folks said: 'Whassup - cat got yer tongue?!'

To Counting Spells

Two people out of three can't spell:
That's S, P, E, then double L.

It all makes sense, at least to me,
That spelling's good for one in three.

An odder thought, more paramount:
Three people out of two can't count!

Nice Is Really Nice! – Martin Killips
(Where you MIGHT learn some French!)

When Pussy Cat is fast asleep,
The world of Mice is quite complete;
For that is when the Mice will play,
Without a care throughout the day;
For through the night Cat's on the beat -
But daytime finds our Cat ASLEEP!

So if the pantry's open wide
Our Mice are prone to pop inside
And cut themselves a slice of cake –
The sort that kindly Grannies bake,
With lots of fruit and crunchy nuts;
(One Mouse will point, another cuts!)
And other Mice will gorge on oats,
Which causes thirst as water bloats
The bellies of our thirsty Mice
(Which sounds quite cute – but isn't nice!)

And while they feast and play and dance
Our Cat is dreaming he's in France;
The Southern part, the French call Nice -
(They say eet so eet rhymes wizz peace!)
I've heard it whispered, high and low,
That Mice don't wish it said quite so;

That they prefer it spoken: 'Nice -
And NOT,' they said, 'because we're MICE!'
But let us leave the Cat at peace
In that small town zee French call Nice
And concentrate on what Mice eat
When Pussy Cat IS FAST ASLEEP!

I think I mentioned they like cake
(The sort that kindly Grannies bake)
And also how their tummies bloat
When they have nibbled lots of oats;

But they won't stop at oats and cake –
The punch bowl soon becomes a lake
Of lemonade and juicy fruit,
(And rest assured now - that IS cute!)
And some will swim while others sip
And even try to build a ship;
What fun and joy is theirs to keep
While Pussy Cat is fast asleep!

But as the sun decides to fall
And shadows slip across the hall;
The Mice, collectively all know
That it is time for them to go.

But they have one last thing to do
Before their slumber's overdue;
For deep asleep upon the mat
Is STILL the sleeping Pussy Cat;
So all the Mice will gather round
And take one whisker they have found
And with a 'One! Two! Three!' they shout
And try to pull the whisker out!

Then 'OUCH!' - the Pussy Cat awakes,
And rubs his whiskers where it aches,
And looks about with puzzled face -
But all the Mice have left the place;
So with a shrug he's off and out

To wander, nightly, all about;
While soft and deep in gentle trance
The Mice are dreaming they're in France;
The Southern part, the French call Nice
(Which you recall should rhyme with peace!)
But if you wake the sleeping Mice
They'll tell you, Nice is really Nice!

Hypochondriac!

I am a hypochondriac - I suffer all life's ills;
I rattle if you shake me as I'm loaded up with pills;
I spend a lot of time in bed because I'm feeling low,
for sickness always ails me - and I want the world to know!

I had a **scarlet** fever and another which is **yellow**,
and once a death, described as **black**, it made me not so well. Oh!
The list of coloured illnesses I've had, you should have seen;
I've even suffered envy - which you know is coloured **green**!

I've had…
Lurgy, scurvy, topsy-turvy,
elephantiasis made me curvy;
Small pox, chicken pox, sheep pox too -
Ella Fitzgerald even made me **blue!**

I've had…
Measles twice and rickets once –
repeatedly, incontinence!

Diabetes, acne, crabs,
leprosy (with weeping scabs);
Whooping cough and Hong Kong flu,
diarrhoea: run to loo!
Haemorrhoids (that's awful piles);
sit and scream - be heard for miles!
Now THAT'S the pain you can't ignore –
SEE THE TEETH MARKS ON MY DOOR!

I've had…
Caries, scabies, even rabies,
neurosyphilis gave me tabés;
Sepsis, prolepsis, stypsis: STOP!
Myxomatosis even made me hop!

I understand amnesia and forgetting are the same -
although when I possessed them I could not recall their name!
And please don't call me immature or even think me brash -
but I'm the only adult that I know with nappy rash!

I've had...
UTI and STD then PMS and BSE
RSI and double A - I even suffered Y2K!
For I'm a hypochondriac whose days are full of woe,
I'm happy in my misery - and I want the World to know!

Just A Minute!

(Author's note: This poem should take precisely one minute to read!)

T.S. Eliot, in a minute, said there's time,
for decisions and revisions which a minute can entwine;
Disaster takes a minute for the San Andreas Faults,
and Chopin thought a minute was sufficient for a waltz!
Even Rudyard Kipling filled his *unforgiving* minute
with sixty single seconds and the earth and all that's in it;
A fool from his money every minute will be torn -
as Barnum said: *'A sucker, every minute's surely born!'*
To Mister Stoker's Dracula whose heart would more than ache
if he were served some garlic with his *bloody minute* steak;
For me to read this rhyme a minute's silence won't occur -
although you might well argue it is what you much prefer;
And so I now will leave you whilst I have your timely ear
with just one final sample where a minute might bring cheer;
By taking you to *Woolworth's*, where I caused great caboodles,
by asking for just *half* a pack, of their *two* minute noodles!

Ron McKinnon

Ron McKinnon is a hard working Aussie dedicated to community work. A tireless friend and organiser, Ron has uniquely captured the experience of the Aussie male seeking 'asylum' in the back yard shed.

Opening time at the Garage

It's Tuesday. Any Tuesday will do. 4pm. Two elderly men met. One weaved his way through the gum trees, the other came across the dusty part of the road jokingly referred to as the zebra crossing. Each carried an object. The garage door was closed. They stopped outside. Then the door began to rise. 'Are you waiting?' asked a third man.

'Just waiting for opening time.' The chairs were ready. The mixed bunch got down to business. One man had fought on the other side in WWII. The other two had fought together. 'These aren't screwtops,' said one of the men. 'Where's the bottle opener?' 'Where did you get that glass?' 'Here you might as well take his bottle opener – you have everything else of his.' The scene was set – two against one. An hour later the bottled beer was gone. Out came the XXXX cans. No need for the bottle opener. One man leaves and returns with a dark green bottle, a light green bottle and 2 trays of ice cubes. There was smothered laughter and bravado. It wasn't long before the last bottle was empty. 'Your tea is ready,' yelled a female voice. 'Yes, ma'am,' said the man who'd been addressed, standing like a well behaved schoolboy. The other two laughed. 'Are you going to take the dog for a walk?' asked the female voice. The laughter stopped. 'What does YOUR wife say?' the third man was asked.6 pm. The two visiting men rushed home. One veered between the gum trees, one tried to find the 'zebra' crossing. When the two looked back the garage door was closed. Anyone passing by would never know three elderly men had passed a marvellous two hours there.

Peter Bullock

Peter Bullock grew up in country Australia with a firsthand knowledge of isolation and ingenuity. He relates his experiences with an eccentric group of hard working men in the days when improvisation was not just a necessity but a national sport.

Woodcutting and "gelly"

When my twin brother John and I were about eleven or twelve we would go out with our father every few weeks to get wood. We had three younger brothers and a sister but they were excused from hard labour on account of us being the eldest. At that time, and for years to come, Mum and Dad had a wood stove, an old Metters No. 3. We also had a chip heater in the bathroom and a copper tub in the washhouse heated by fire, so wood was an integral factor in our energy needs. In fact, we only used electricity for lights, the radio and the fridge.

We used to go out to the 54 mile peg on the Albany Highway, generally with our Uncle Harry along as well. His name was Henry, but he was called Harry as they used to in those days. Most times we would return to find a dead tree on the ground that had been reconnoitred the last time we'd been out. My brother John and I would attack it with a 12 ft crosscut saw. While John and I were sawing away Dad and Harry would be splitting and loading the trailer as well as Harry's Austin Ute. When they'd finished loading Dad and Harry would head off to their respective houses to unload. By the time they got back John and I would have the next load three quarters cut. Dad and Harry would split and load up what we'd cut then go scout about to find a couple of trees for the next trip.

When John and I finished we'd go for a wander with the 22 to see if we could find a roo (kangaroo) and when we arrived back at the site all the wood would be loaded and we'd have a cup of tea and head off home. That was a typical wood-cutting trip.

Uncle Harry lived in Jandakot in the stationmaster's house. The station had been closed and there was no longer a Station Master—he'd left to work on the railways as a "snake-charmer", that's what they called fettlers in those days as they frequently encountered snakes and had to deal with them. Harry had bought a 5 acre block about half a mile from where we lived and retired as he was getting on a bit. He was the oldest of thirteen kids and Dad was the youngest.

On Harry's block there was a big dead jarrah log on the ground that was about five feet diameter. One day he decided we'd get an easy load of wood, so the old man got some gelignite or "gelly" as it was known—four sticks with detonators and fuse. We hammered some wedges into the fallen tree and put the sticks of gelly in different parts. Then we measured the fuse to get as close to an even fire as we could, lit the fuses and pissed off a fair way to let nature do its course.

Well, when the gelly went off it blew the log into big long chunks about as thick as you'd want for firewood. The only trouble with that was, it was impossible to saw the sharp blocks so we had to load up the trailer and take the timber home and bust them all into short lengths with the axe. I'll tell you what for nothing—for an "easy" load of wood it was the hardest work we had ever done. Me and my brother weren't impressed, but it was a bloody good explosion.

By crikey, we were glad when the old man bought a Mobilco circular saw on wheels! A 4 cylinder car motor provided the grunt. It was even better later on when Dad and Harry got a 6ft Blue Moon two-man chainsaw that they shared. Then, when we were about sixteen, I headed down to Lake King to work on a farm, and John went to Wave Hill Station to work there. After we boys left home Dad bought a Mculloch 18" chain saw, what a great thing that was, but no use to John or me.

Growing up then was fun. I would like to be back there now, but I'd want a chainsaw with me.

Cracker night on Mulberry Farm

When I was a child the second most important date of the year, after Christmas, was the 5th of November. Cracker Night. For a couple of months before that all the neighbourhood kids would be busy constructing bonfires on our verges.

We lived south east of Fremantle in a suburb called Davis Park that was built in 1950 for the baby boom and consequently most houses had between two and eight children in them. But it was universally known as Mulberry Farm after the original settlers' farm here.

There were a lot of mulberry trees and almond trees down the road from us, where the South Fremantle High School is now. Behind us, there was a limestone quarry, a large cross country Harley Scramble track and market gardens, then a fair bit of bush, probably around 500 acres.

These are the places where we gathered anything burnable for our bonfire, often dragging it home on our billy carts. Now our street was fairly long, so there were about three bonfires on the street. We had one in front of our house and on the night the kids around us and their parents would gather at our bonfire.

As the night got closer we kids would sneak out at night pilfering material from other bonfires (we called it rustling) as it was a point of pride to have the biggest one, and the other kids would do the same to us, so there tended to be a fair bit of movement of boys and material at night. We also kept busy creating Guy Fawkes effigies to burn on top of the bonfire.

As it approached dark on the eagerly awaited night we would bring our crackers out. When Dad gave us the nod we'd light the bonfire and start letting crackers off. There were Tom Thumbs, Halfpenny bombs and the big Four Penny Bombs that could blow a milk bottle to smithereens. We had Jumping Jacks, Golden Showers, Roman Candles, Catherine Wheels and Sky Rockets among others. We'd light a Jumping Jack and chuck it among the sheilas.

Crikey didn't they squeal and shout! We nailed Catherine Wheels to the fence posts and let them off. We stuck Sky Rockets in beer bottles—with a hiss and a plume of fire away they'd go! Sometimes a bottle fell over and the rocket would scream along parallel to the ground. If it hit a fence it would ricochet randomly.

Then adults and kids scattered in all directions. I must admit most times the bottle fell over it wasn't a complete accident. Eventually the fire got to the Guy Fawkes effigy sitting at the top and it went up in a blaze of glory.

We cheered and yelled like billio! While the effigy burned we chanted; 'Remember, remember the fifth of November, the gunpowder treason and plot'. There were a couple more lines but they've gone in the mists of time.

At the end of the night we roasted potatoes in the embers. We used a garden rake to drag the spuds out when they were done and many a rake met its demise on bonfire night.

The next morning we would get up as early as possible and scavenge all the bonfire sites in the district collecting the duds and fizzogs and dropped crackers, including those whose wicks had gone out after they were chucked.

We generally found enough to keep us going for a couple more days. Then it was all over for another year, but when you're a young kid a year is a bloody long time. It was all good fun. I know why cracker night was banned and I agree with the reasons but I'm bloody glad it happened after I was a kid.

Peter Bullock

It was a good time. It was a time in our Australian history when we were reminded what the 5th of November meant to us. Even though it was English history it was entwined with our system of government and the history of the people who settled here.

Marilyn Linn

Marilyn Linn enjoys writing short stories and poems, some of which have been published in Australia, New Zealand, Japan and USA. Marilyn is currently writing a children's novella. She is a member of Seaside Writers' group, Marion Writers' Group and Bindii-the SA Japanese poetry form group.

Valley of the Winds

The air was chilly and a heavy covering of dew formed thin ice on the fence posts, car bonnets and our flimsy tent. Our camping gear was packed as we planned to go on to Kata Tjuta after we had driven around Uluru.

We were up early enough to see the magic of the sunrise over Uluru, along with many other seekers of the sunrise. It was magnificent. When most of the tourists had moved off as the sun rose in the pale blue sky, we drove around the seven kilometre base, stopping at the various waterholes and plaques to read the stories of the Rock.

Our next stop was Kata Tjuta, the many headed conglomerate of rocks rising out of the desert of the Northern Territory. Kata Tjuta was formally known as The Olgas, named after a Queen of Spain in 1872 when the rocks were first seen by white men. The Aboriginal stories identify the highest mound, Mount Olga, as the home of the snake Wanambi, who, during the rainy season, stays curled up in the waterhole.

In the dry season, Wanambi crawls through the caves. His breath is the wind which blows through the gorges. When he gets angry the wind becomes a hurricane.

We had all day, so we took our time with morning tea, packed a bit of lunch and some water in our well-used backpacks and headed off to explore this bunch of rocks.

As the sun rose higher, the heat of the desert made us cling to the shady edges of the rocks. We seemed to be walking in circles and soon all the rocks began to look the same to me. I was hot and getting bored with looking at red earth, red rocks and red dust as the wind whipped up little whirly winds around our feet.

By the time the sun was overhead I had had enough of the life of the adventurer but my intrepid partner, Geoff, was just getting interested.

I deliberately dillydallied over our meagre sandwiches at lunch and declared we should have a quick siesta before heading off again, hopefully, back to the car and out of this hot dusty place, but I was out of luck. We trudged on.

The wind was getting quite strong and was howling mournfully through the gaps. I knew this was called the Valley of the Winds, so I should have been prepared for the haunting sound. But I wasn't and I began to get a little scared.

'Get a grip,' declared Geoff, when I expressed my desire to leave this place.

'Do you actually know where we are? I mean, really know how to get out of this spooky place?' I asked coldly.

'Of course I do.'

So on we trudged. By now the sun had gone over the rocks and it was getting cool. Shadows lengthened and dark pockets formed in crevices and caves. The wind continued to gust and throw sand in my eyes.

'Are we nearly out of here yet?' I asked, sounding like a bored child on a long car trip.

'We are nearly. Just up here a bit there should be a wider valley and we can go out there.'

Geoff and I have had many arguments about the word 'should'. If it 'should' my experience was that it never did. This time was no exception.

Darkness now seemed to be covering us with a heavy purple blanket and I could see no way out of this heap of stones. I was tired, hungry, thirsty and just a little bit afraid that we were lost.

After some time, I refused to go any further. I sat on a small mound and remembered the snake, Wanambi. We wouldn't even see a snake in this darkness.

'Snakes don't come out at night and especially when it is cold,' snapped Geoff.

'I am glad you have noticed that it is cold and night,' I snapped back. 'We are lost, aren't we?'

'Well, we might have taken a wrong turn but I think we should be able to get out up here a bit.'

There was that 'should' again.

We wandered around for a while, until the sliver of the new moon arrived over the red rock mounds.

'You are right,' Geoff finally conceded, 'we are lost. I think we should stay where we are for tonight and get our directions straight in the morning when the sun comes up.'

'You think what? Where are we going to sleep? I don't see any motels here and our tent is in the car.' I was not amused.

'There is a little cave just up here. We can huddle in there. I know it might not be too comfortable, but it will be dry.'

I was too flabbergasted to speak. My silence spoke louder than any words could have. He was very apologetic, and so he ought to be. Here we were, in the middle of a heap of big rocks, in the middle of the desert, with no food, no beds and only light clothing, and the squalling wind was cold and threatening. It threatened to frighten me to death! So I huddled in the cave as close as I could get to Geoff, wanting the warmth of his body and the strength of his arms to protect me from Wanambi.

In the distance a dingo called to its mate. I had read that the pointed rocks in the east are the rock of Malu, the kangaroo man, who is dying from wounds inflicted by dingoes. Silently, I begged the dingoes to go away.

'That must be the east,' I whispered to Geoff.

He was asleep! How could he be asleep? Every nerve in my body was on edge and he was sleeping. My protector! I was so angry with him.

I shivered with savage thoughts of my husband and what was going to happen to him in the morning. The cold and the restless moaning of the wind echoing around the rocks kept me wide awake.

After a long and cold night, a few rays of sun ventured out. I eased myself to my feet, trying not to disturb Geoff. My limbs were frozen stiff. My head ached and my temper was boiling. Geoff slept on. What a nerve he had.

I crept out of our dirty little cave and looked around. He had been nearly right. There was the wide chasm he had been looking for before it got dark.

Not very gently, I shook his arm to rouse him. He had a stunned look on his face as he regained consciousness in waking. He had forgotten where we were!

'Get up and come and look here,' I demanded.

He was stiff too, but got no mercy from me.

'Look! There's the opening I knew was here somewhere.'

He pointed to the opening. The triumphant tone in his voice did nothing to ease my anger.

'Just get me out of here. I am tired, cold and hungry.'

Within a few minutes we were out of the Valley of the Winds and back at our car. I put on as many warm clothes as I could find without unpacking everything and we got in the car. Neither of us in the mood to chat.

The heater in the car thawed the icy atmosphere, as we headed back to Uluru to make some hot food and a cuppa, before we headed out to King's Canyon.

The Call of the Wild

We were camping in the Gammon Ranges, in South Australia. Our group comprised of 12 people in four tents; three of those people were children aged between 12 and 14 years. Our camp was in a wide clearing near a natural spring with assorted eucalypts and low scrubby plants around it.

Our first clue that we had night-time thieves was when our bread had gone missing from our annexe several mornings in a row. Apples had been stolen from one of the other tents.

One night as we sat around our small campfire, watching myriad stars and satellites move across the high dark sky, we heard a dingo howl. It sounded near but we couldn't see anything outside our firelight. From the distance, we heard an answering call. Dingoes don't bark. They use their howl for all communications – calling to establish which dog is where, a warning to any intruders, including humans, claiming territory or to tell of a food source it had found.

We continued talking and not long after, another mournful howl came, much closer this time. The children were afraid, but we felt sure the wild dog wouldn't come any closer.

But we were wrong. A thin, honey-coloured dog, about the size of a Kelpie, emerged from the scrub. We could see it was a female with a half-grown pup. They quietly circled our camp as we watched. She dragged a back leg and had a wound on her side. We knew that we shouldn't encourage interaction but, with her pup, she was drawing closer and closer. We sat motionless as she came into the firelight.

When she and her pup were inside our circle of chairs, she lay down and her pup sat beside her. His coat was slightly darker than hers and he was in good condition. Dingoes and people watched each other. After several minutes, one of the men went and returned with a piece of bread, which he tossed towards the female dingo. She didn't move, but her pup grabbed the bread hungrily. Then he sat again. Not wanting to frighten the dogs, we eventually moved off to our tents as quietly as we could. They showed no fear or aggression.

Morning came, and as we staggered out of our tents into the brilliant Gammon Ranges morning sun, we were surprised to see the two dogs still there. The campfire had long ago gone out but they lay, curled together. With people moving around we were cautious of our new camping friends and gave them a wide berth. As the morning routines got underway, the kettle boiled, people talked and cooked toast on the gas barbecue, the dogs just watched. It seemed a natural thing to toss a few crusts to them and they ate quickly, but didn't get up to move on. We finished our morning rituals, secured our camp as much as we felt was necessary and headed out for a day of exploration.

We returned about 4:00pm, as we usually did, and the dingoes were sitting close to one of the tents. They had been into our annexe again, evidenced by the now empty bread packet on the ground. Keeping an eye on them at all times, little groups prepared to cook their evening meals. The smell of barbecue filled the air as the sun sent long shadows over our campsite.

After we had eaten and cleaned up, we built our little fire and drew the chairs around in a circle. Still the dingoes sat and watched, ears always pricked. For some time we ignored them. We were surprised when they again crept into the circle of light and warmth and sat down. The female's injury looked bad, and we were concerned about her, but could do nothing. The pup was alert and curious. He edged his way closer to our feet, creeping on his belly or taking a cautious step occasionally.

The pup was as cute as any puppy could be, alert, with fearless eyes. One of the men put out his hand, offering a piece of cake, and the pup came to get it. He didn't run away, but stood and consumed it there. The female watched, not getting up. Another camper clicked his fingers and offered the pup some fat from a leftover chop. The pup enjoyed that, too. This cheeky young dog worked his way around the circle, getting bits and pieces from various people.

Eventually, we made our way to our tents, leaving the dingoes by the dying fire embers. Late in the night I heard a low howl and thought the dingoes must be leaving. Momentarily, I felt a passing sadness. It was a rare experience to have wild animals come in to make friends.

I arose early next morning, while the sky was silver grey, and a chilly mist hung low over the nearby water. At first I couldn't see the dogs and assumed they had departed, but then a slight movement caught my eye and I stood still. It was the pup and he was alone. He came over to me and I didn't know what to do. At first I was reluctant to feed him so I bent forward, my empty hand outstretched, and he came to me. He licked my hand as any friendly dog would, and I spoke softly to him. He watched while I got him a piece of the bacon waiting to be cooked. With no fear, he sat close by while I got the barbecue going and began cooking. Others of our group emerged for their breakfast and the young dingo was well fed. But we couldn't see the mother.

After breakfast, a small group went for a walk and on their return, reported finding the female dog, dead, not far away. The discovery dampened our spirits for a while and we wondered what would happen to the pup. He was unconcerned, playing with a fluttering dry leaf nearby. We again tidied the camp and prepared to head out for the day on the long, gibber-strewn road. The pup sat a short distance away and watched. Then he did a couple of puppy bounces and he walked up the long road, a diminishing figure, silhouetted against the scarlet tendrils of the rising sun, fore-runners creeping across the sky from a determined and hopeful dawn.

Asparagus

Down the yard, by the back fence Grandpa built a dunny.
It was built on a bit of a slope and always looked quite funny.

In the evening the spiders hung around
and the mice came out to play.
The path was littered with leaves and twigs
not such a problem by day.

But I was a kid, not a brave big man and I dreaded going 'for walks',
until I found Grandpa, shickered, amongst the asparagus stalks.

His tongue hung out from his dribbly mouth,
his eyes were roaming freely,
He'd staggered along the slippery path
trying to balance unsuccessfully.

There he was, flat on his back he'd been heading for his shed.
No-one dared go there, it was approached with deep, dark dread.

In his shed, Grandpa kept all kinds of strange things,
like bottles of grog and tobacco.
He kept tins of nails and jars with string,
he was like some poor homeless hobo.

It seemed the asparagus had tipped him fair on his face in the dirt,
he cussed and struggled, made for the dunny- definitely not alert.

He reached the shed where he fell through the doorway
colliding with a huge rat,
He was found next day, asleep on some hay,
he claimed the rat was under his hat.
The moral of this story is, the dunny was too far away, so
when Grandpa was feeling better, (he was giving up booze,)
no-one really believed him, because he was such a babbler.

Marilyn Linn

He said he was moving the long-drop, closer to the house.
Out came the post-hole digger,
to make the holes deeper and bigger.

He built a new loo, with a double seat as well,
a door was not something he needed,
his garden was the favoured view,
he planted seeds randomly and hardly ever weeded.

When the dunny was rebuilt and Grandpa happy,
Grandma made a decision, she knew where the garden could go.
While Grandpa was in his shed, blotto again, no doubt,
she called in a mate with a big yellow back hoe.

The bloke with the truck and back hoe,
cleared out the back yard with glee,
out went the radishes, asparagus and kale,
Grandma said, 'Come in, I'll make you some tea.'

Grandpa staggered out of his wonky old shed,
'What the hell do ya' think ya' doin'?
You've spoiled my secret ambition,
 I've wanted to do that for years.'

After some cake and a cuppa,
Grandma and Grandpa were dancing around,
they were singing and having a grand time,
Until Grandpa slipped on an asparagus tip . . .
Grandma stood back, folded her arms and frowned.

Victoria Norton

Victoria Norton is studying a Degree in Creative Writing, and writing her debut novel. Victoria has been published in *We Are Australian*; *Write On!*; *Writers Voice*, the FAW magazine; *Hunter Professional Arts*; *The Ness Fireside Book of God, Ghosts and Ghouls*; *Waltzing Matilda* and *Australian Literary Review* Online Magazine.

The Cockie's Mother & the Hired Hand

I see you there, old woman, in the grey shade of the veranda. I hear your sleeping breath. I'm curious as to what it would take to wake you, a prod or a word. I'll roll a quick durry while I'm here in the cool.

That rattan chair fits you like a second skin, do you sit there often? I don't get to sit much in my working day. What's it like to while away the time?

The bush flies are biting the skin on me face and arms. I've rolled me worn-thin flanno sleeves tight on me biceps to protect me upper arms. They're hard and strong from yakka hard and long. Flies're buzzin' around your face old woman. I can hardly stand to listen to the sawing sound that hits me ears with such discomfort. Me hearing is sensitive. I think from the drumming of the shears, the rousties yelling over each other as they muster the mob in the catching pens and shed. Kelpie dogs barking all day, showing their excitement as they herd and climb on the backs of the soon-to-be-shorn sheep.

All of 'em doin' what they love best. When I'm away from that, it hurts to have even a quiet sound. An insect, for its tiny size, bothers me more than anything. Yeah, they annoy the buggery out of me. But you don't seem to mind.

I wonder what I taste like to a fly right now, covered as I am in the stink of the fresh-cut wool clip, sheep shit and piss, and the blood from the merino's folds that even my well trained shears couldn't avoid. I've wiped a thick stained strip down the sides of me baggy jeans, wiping off the blood and the sweat and the lanolin sticky with heat. Me boots are heavy and hot. At night they stay outside the shearer's dorm, a bloke couldn't breathe with 'em in the room. Lined up outside the fly-screened doors on the long veranda, the reek from ten pairs of shearer's boots would be enough to kill a squadron of soldiers. You always have a spare pair, one day on, one day off.

We many-booted shearers visit here just once a year and always move along to another shearer's dorm, another long veranda and another stinking shed. Under me arms the sweat has dried on me shirt to a firm, stiff, stinking crust. I change me flanno's twice in a shearing day that lasts from dawn til dusk. Sometimes I carry on with the job shirtless but for a bluey.

It gets bloody hot in the sheds – you're wiping sweat from yer brow all day. Sometimes I just toss a shirt in the bin when you know it'll never wash up clean again. I can't smell meself at all by the end of the day. The smells from others, stinking even more than me, fill and stuff me nose and throat. No use complaining, we all have to rub along, pong or no pong.

The wool fat is smooth on me hands and I rub it into me arms and elbows – skin scaly thin and bones pointy with age. It sure does keep your skin supple even as yer thighs burn and yer back breaks from bending over the clippers.

At least the combs and cutters are electric now. But I learned me trade on the blades, and there was a lot more blood and tar in them days. Now it's a squirt of brown anti-septic and away they go. The hot tar was cruel, even as we knew it stopped the rot of fresh-cut flesh we still hated to use it. A crying sheep is a sad, sad thing and while you might not think it, we respect their right to a safe, kind life. Unless it's dinner time and anyone of us would do the necessary. In a kind way, a quick, deep cut to a stretched out neck. The Cockie's wives or camp cooks stew the mutton, corn a leg or roast a joint. Ten blokes like me can get through a powerful amount of meat in a meal.

I've long been called the ringer, gunning 300 and more head a day, but I'm not first out of the shed today – I'm last. Instead they called me stagger in the shed today. They know I'm passed it. I'm here for me pay. I have to decide – to wake her or not. Or go look for the Cockie's office.

I'll spend most of me pay in the pub. We all do. Makes you real thirsty, does shearing. This life encourages great bursts of excess, food and grog and forty rollies a day. Women used and left bruised by promises never meant to be kept. Not the life for a married man, not the life if you have kids to support. Although some of us, not me mind, some of us have a left a stork's parcel and moved on to a new girl, leaving the poor girl alone to bring up the left over offspring.

I'll finish me walk to the Cockie's office. As I walk I stretch to relieve the tight spasms across my shoulders. This'll be my last year shearing. I'm old and broken and it's too hard to keep up. Me youthful exuberance and physical stamina are gone. I missed the chance at a family, I wouldn't have made a good job of it anyway. I'm too set in me ways to share and live with give and take. I'll miss me mates, that's for sure. You sure do look lonely old woman.

I see you there, old man, in the dappled shade of the wisteria vine.

I hear your ragged whistling breath, emphysemic from your White Ox rollies. Just like my Malcolm smoked. The pungent tobacco smoke hovers with a life of its own, stirring memories I'd rather bury than relive.

My hands have rubbed my chair arms smooth over time. For sixty years, longer than you've been alive, I've sat here. Every single day. But not for wasting time. Anxiously watching the bush fire on the horizon, wondering will the wind turn and burn us out? Smelling the rain on its way, the air crisp to breathe and bright with lightening flashes, waiting for the first heavy drops to ping on the red iron-rich dirt of the home yard and release the mineral tainted tang. Or, counting the days of the big dry, coughing dust from willy-willies dancing by. Waiting for the long drove to be over, will he come home safe? A pregnancy long overdue, will this baby ever come? The children playing away from the house, will they toy with danger? How long will it take for my husband to die? Yes, this chair is the repository of my life story. Here I'm reminded of the fearful times; the angry times, the loving and the sad. This cane has soaked up all the stories of my life, yet it holds me now, close and comforting. Every memory brighter as I age, the early days so poignant even as I reminisce I fight back tears. I had so much, and I lost so much.

The flies don't bother me. The droning is mostly in the background. Living to be eighty in the bush you hear a lot of flies, and you learn to live with them. They probably followed your scent trail from the shearing shed to the veranda. I smell the sheep on you old man. The astringent stench is so pungent I can taste the sharpness on my tongue. You really stink old man – of work and hasty smokos, and tannin from tea drunk strong and sweet to keep you focused. The sweat on your hat will never stop stinking, each man stinks in his own way. My husband stank, his hat and his clothes, but it changed with the lung cancer. Then his body smelled of the drugs he was given, of the poison in his body. But I sure do miss the smell of him now. If I try and recall it I cry, silently at night, so as not to wake my son. Grief is a life time of waiting for the pain to go away. I think of the smell of him, more than the sound of him, more than the look of him and I cry.

I don't want to talk to you. Hurry and pass on by. Since the Parkinson's the tremor makes my body shake and my mouth changes the sound of the words I want to say. When my words fall on familiar ears I am understood, but oh, it's so embarrassing with strangers.

Even my face has changed shape. My Malcolm would never recognise me now. He used to hold my face in his hands and gently kiss each feature. 'My Love,' he'd say – he always called me 'Love.' He'd say 'My Love, your eyes are like sapphires, your nose like a button, and your lips like a rose'. Oh, he spoke with such a broad outback accent, yet his poetry was most private and only for me, a contradiction for sure. The other blokes would have had a go at him if they knew he had such a tender side. Malcolm said I was his light, his beacon. Ah, I wish he was here. He was my light, too. I didn't know that until he was gone. I should have thanked him.

Poor Malcolm, hands so hard and calluses rough, they'd break my thin, sun-abused skin on his touch. His hands with cuts and bruises, thumbnails black from blows from miss-timed farming tools. Ah, his farm-hard hands. So strong, despite the injuries, always there to pick me up, to hold me tight. The last touch of his hand on my face is seared like a hot white brand into my memory. I feel it now.

Where you stand old man, hundreds have stood before. This cool dark place is not just for you. Children played on rainy days, and winter days when frost crackled underfoot while their mothers scrubbed my floors. Shed hands, cooks, classers and even the dogs have made that space their own from time to time.

My nose twitches and I want to rub my nostrils to make the itchy sensation go away, but then you'll see I'm awake and aware that you're standing there. I don't want to be rude, but can you move along please.

My son isn't here, can't you tell by now. Are you going to stay here all day? Get round to the office and collect your pay, that's what you came for, right?

Feel that? I know from years of sitting here that he shifted his weight from one foot to the other. It causes a pressure wave that moves along the old tongue and groove floor. Hear that? Creaking, the rotting wood strains from the tension. It seems to take the longest time, but eventually he moves off with a scuffle and a clunk and then all is silent. My last thought as I feel real deep sleep take my mind and my body: Is he lonely as lonely as me?

Linda Ruth Brooks

Linda has written a *Curious & Inelegant Childhood* and several fiction novels. She has written and illustrated children's books and been published in various anthologies. Her published books include the genres of fiction, nonfiction and poetry.

"Steptoe and Son"

Emma arrived at 43 Pleasant Street and moaned. The street name was crooked and the house looked like it should be condemned. It had been painted a nauseating yellow half a century ago, and whatever window frames had once graced the house's exterior were long gone. She parked outside.

Mr Fenwick was a new patient, just released from the local hospital after a prolonged stay. She groaned. The nursing notes were patchy—'Frail Aged' didn't give much information. Well, it shouldn't take too long; she only had to bath and dress him, then check his Webster medication packs.

The interior lived up to the promise of the exterior; it was a living breathing disaster area. A large woman beckoned Emma inside from an ancient armchair with a hasty gesture. She didn't get up or exert herself to open the door. Emma pushed the sliding door aside. It gave an unwelcome screech.

''e's in there,' said the woman, pointing to a partly obscured doorway. 'Waiting for 'is bath 'e is. Hates to be kep' waitin'.'

'That's b'cause it's all a man 'as left to do in life,' bellowed a distant voice.

Emma quickly surveyed the living room, although this was a poor description because it was more like a maze. Piles of women's magazines were stacked in three feet high columns that looked a shade precarious. The rest of the room was furnished with random lounge chairs that had seen a few decades of wear and tear, and were also piled up with a variety of bric-a-brac.

'Git a move on. I aint got all day,' said the voice. 'Oh, bloody hell, *I* 'ave got all day, aint I? A man'd be better off dead.'

'Yeah, well. Shuffle off then, ya miserable git,' muttered a tall slender man in his early twenties as he flew past Emma. When he reached the haven of the patio, which looked like a corner of the local tip, he began to chain smoke and read the newspaper.

'Did y'put 20 bucks on No Hoper?' laughed the raspy voice from the bedroom. This speech brought on an attack of wheezing reminiscent of some old codger out of a Dickens' novel.

'Oh ullo, y'here at last,' he said, when Emma came into the room. 'Not another bloody new one.'

'Now Pa. Be nice to the nurse. We can't have them refusing to come, *again,* y'know,' said his wife. She briefly looked up from her Woman's Day. ''e uses the commode first, dear.'

Albert Fenwick possessed a beak of a nose that dominated his face, perhaps because his face was gaunt and his frame skeletal. Emma felt she was on the set of Steptoe and Son. Except for the addition of the dumpy sister of Hyacinth Bucket from 'Keeping up Appearances' sitting there as well.

'Good Lord, will y'look at the size of this one. Could fit 'er in y'pocket. How y'gonna lift me around, sweetheart. Did y'bring a crane?' This statement was followed by another wheezing session that clearly exhausted him as much as it amused him.

''E's got newmoania,' said his wife knowledgeably. ''Avin' an 'ell of a time, 'e is, poor love.'

'I c'n speak f'meself woman!' yelled Albert.

'Y'don' 'ave t'yell. Y've got good blooming lungs for a man with emphyseemiah.' She sat back, satisfied she'd explained the medical realities. ''is chart's over there, love,' she said, pointing to a corner of the room that couldn't possibly have been accessed in the last decade. 'But I c'n tell y'what t'do. I looked after 'im m'self 'til m'knees give out.'

Emma sighed. There was no way she could get to the dusty table, much less sort through the mess to find his notes. *If* they existed, which she was beginning to doubt.

Emma checked the bathroom while he finished his morning beer. Judging by the debris in the house, this was a staple part of their diet. The bath was accessible and well set up. The occupational therapist had done her job well. After helping him onto the commode she went to set up for his bath. He was amazingly spry and hadn't needed more than a guiding hand to get out of bed and sit. Being naked from the waist down had made things easier. Emma was no more surprised by that than the dried food on his poorly buttoned pyjama coat.

She arranged the bath according to his wife's rambling instructions, and was just about to go back for Albert when he came flying past her like a clanking streak of misery. There was a flapping piece of toilet paper hanging from between his buttocks. Instinctively Emma grabbed it, but just as she swiped the paper away and reached for his bony arm, he went down like a bag of bones.

'Oh Good Lord, not again!' said his wife.

Emma was mortified. Her first day with him and he'd fallen. The brief care notes had omitted that he had the tendency to bolt like the greyhounds he betted on.

'Oh God! Claris!' he wheezed. 'Me coccyx! I done broke it orf!'

Emma reached down to help him, but he waved her away. His drama scene wasn't over yet. Claris made a token effort to get up, but was firmly wedged between the armrests in the timber chair. Helplessly Emma turned back to 'Steptoe' to help him, but he was up and off again like greased lightning. With a half gallop, half limp he careened towards the bathroom.

Emma managed to get one hand under his right arm, but the gesture was useless. This skinny streak was too fast for her. He threw first one leg, and then the other over the bath, before plonking down with a satisfied splash. Once there, he allowed Emma to suds his body with evident delight.

'That's great. I love a good hard scrub,' he murmured, casting her a sly look, '...but God help me, me bum 'urts...'

He was going to milk this for all it was worth. By now Emma knew he'd done no real harm, but if it was drama he wanted - drama he'd get. 'Better have an X-ray if it's that bad, Albert. Maybe I should send you to hospital to get checked out,' she said.

'D'ya want me to call an amblance?' piped up Claris, perhaps sensing a few day's peace.

'That'd be bloody right,' cursed Albert. 'Wouldn't leave y'bloody magazine to wash yer own 'usband what's stood by yer through thick and thin, but yer c'n rouse y'self to get rid o' me.'

By some miracle Claris had dislodged herself from the chair and was smoothing her floral dress. 'Thick and thin's right,' she muttered.

'What'd y'say, Claris?'

'I'm just askin' the nurse iffen she'd like a nice 'ot cuppa tea, dear.'

'C'n y'get me a beer when yer go to the fridge, Mum?' called the son, looking up from his paper.

'Say please t'yer mother, yer waste 'o space. And get yer own goddamned beer y'lazy clod. And don't touch mine, yer good f'nothing sloth!'

'Whadya want on the fifth race, Dad?'

'Stuffed if I know. If a man 'ad a chance to look at 'is own paper 'e might be able to tell yer.'

Emma towelled him dry and grabbed his arm securely before he had another chance to bolt. This alone was an effort.

Albert Fenwick had not been endowed with any measure of patience. He gave Emma no time to tie the cords of his pyjama pants so she had to hold the ties, as well as Albert, on the precarious journey back to the room.

She deftly threw clean sheets on the bed while he wheezed in the corner, still slyly regarding her with a watchful eye. Luckily Albert

Fenwick wasn't one of her tyrannical ward sisters of the past, because Emma dispensed with every bed-making rule of nursing.

When he was settled back in bed, Albert's sullen-faced son brought him a beer and the paper.

'Great breakfast Sis! Whadya reckon?' He slanted a glance in Emma's direction as he downed the beer straight from the stubby bottle.

'Well, Albert. I reckon I'll have to up your insulin dose.'

He hooted a wheezing laugh. 'You'll do,' he chortled.

Dad's apprentice

'I'm going to build a shed,' said Dad, over breakfast one Sunday morning.

'But we've already got two sheds Daddy.' I was confused.

I had been my father's apprentice for half a dozen years. I'd begun at the age of five when I discovered my aptitude for 'puddling in the shed', as mum phrased it, was greater than any abilities I possessed for assisting order inside our pristine abode. I began, as all apprentices do, with watching, listening and fetching.

Then I had graduated to cleaning engine parts and holding the torch for Dad to see the deep and secret parts of the car engine. I knew just how important it was for the beam to be steady. There we would be—two heads bent together, wrestling with the problem of repairing tired car engines. However, this construction of a shed was a whole new venture. My mind boggled at the thought. We had a work-shed at the back of the house. It was where all the wonders of machines, ham radios, wrought iron welding, stone polishing and sign making occurred. Then there was the 'back shed' another 100 yards or so down our half acre block, in the shade of the mulberry tree. It housed timber and kindling for the incinerator. It also contained used boards with rusty nails that we kids invariably trod on as we raced through—getting them stuck into our bare feet, or through our shoes. This misadventure would require a trip to the doctor for a tetanus shot.

Our tree-house was next to that shed and we would often lie indolently back, choosing the plumpest mulberries, while the furl and smell of the smoke would rise tantalisingly towards us. Of course, we deserted the tree-house on the days Dad burned old tyres below, where there was a permanent brown patch. Mum often lamented she'd never have lawn there. It was the only blot on her perfect grass, which was watered by Dad's complicated watering system, and she referred to it as 'a blight to the eyes'.

'Never mind Else,' Dad remarked blandly, 'less to do.'

'Humph. Less for *you* to do Max.'

Dad never disputed this fact, he merely smiled sagely.

'Why do we need another shed, Dad? Are y'starting another hobby?' Dad winced at the word 'hobby'. This was often Mum's assessment of his many skills, as if he were a recalcitrant child who had a playroom all to himself, while she 'slaved' over the real jobs.

'Ah,' Dad said, his face alight. 'This "shed" is going to be a garage.'

'Oh my,' I said, my eyes round with wonder. 'Can I help?'

'Thought you'd never ask,' he responded, eyes twinkling.

I gulped my cereal. This was indeed an honour.

'Don't plough through your food, Linda. You'll choke,' said Mum. 'I suppose that means I'll be getting no help today.'

I pleaded with Mum with my eyes—my words so often brought trouble.

'Oh go on, the pair of you. I suppose you'll come back filthy.'

'Of course not, Else. We'll wash up outside,' said Dad.

Mum sighed. Her idea of a proper standard of cleanliness appropriate for entering 'her' house did not match ours. We children had long ago learned the sheds were Dad's and the house was Mum's. Until repairs we needed to the house and then it was 'his'.

When I went outside. I was stunned. There was a pile of bricks, large bags of cement and an old worn-out cement mixer. We didn't own these, so their presence was surprising, but not as surprising as the idea Dad knew anything about their use. I seldom doubted my father's abilities, but that day I did.

I had helped him nail fibro sheets, spackle holes in numerous walls and even handed him plumbing tape and tools when he had laid, or repaired our plumbing. But this was veering into serious construction. Literally from the ground up.

'Oh,' I said, my mind scrambling to understand. 'Have you done this before, Dad?'

'Of course!'

Wasting no time, Dad set about explaining how everything worked, while his long deft fingers used a Stanley knife to slit open the cement bags. I was fascinated by his hands—work-worn, but artistic.

'Run and get the hose, Bub.' Even though I chafed at being called 'bub' at eleven, I ran to bring the hose end to where Dad had meticulously arranged everything. I noticed a pile of sand behind the cement mixer.

'You're not making a sandpit are you, Dad? 'Cause I'm way too old for one, and we'd never hear the end of it from Mum. She says the only thing sandpits are good for is to provide every cat in the neighbourhood with a toilet.'

Dad rolled his eyes. 'We need the sand to mix with the cement.'

'Oh,' I said with some relief. 'Silly me.'

'You weren't to know. You only know what you're told.'

'So what are those long things?' I pointed to long steel rods that swirled like Mum's favourite Liquorice sticks.

'That's reo. It's short for reinforcing. If we don't use it the cement floor will sag and sink and sway.'

Dad's deep voice rumbled as he went through the details, measurements and processes. I smiled, enjoying this aspect of my father. According to Mum, Dad over-explained everything.

'Your father will use twenty words when two would do.'

When it came to the electronic devices in the house the rest of us heartily agreed with this assessment, as we were usually waiting impatiently for Dad to turn something on or tweak it.

'We could well do without all that mumbo jumbo, Max. A person just wants the blooming thing to work, not understand its 'goings on',' Mum would say. This diatribe never worked on Dad, but each of us had begged him to 'leave off' at some time. He would just smile benignly and continue until he finished, even when we pronounced we were 'fed to back teeth' of listening to him. The more impatient we became, the more he chuckled. 'Your father's obsessed with all that gobbledy gook. Mum complained. Everyone kept quiet about her own compulsions.

However, that day I was more than happy to listen to Dad's every word. After all, I'd been let me out of the housework. With Mum happily inside scrubbing everything within an inch of its life, Dad and I mixed cement and laid bricks. I found there was a perfect consistency for cement—an optimum mix of sand and cement powder.

Once it was mixed it was called mortar. I learned that a plumb line, which was a piece of string with a wooden weight made sure the line of bricks was straight and true. I found this part fascinating. I'd been wondering where Dad would find a ruler long enough for a garage.

Dad had already dug the ground for the foundation and had a small trench at the side to lay the bricks because the land was sloped.

At least, that's how I remembered it. I know there was at least one row of bricks I laid, after carefully watching him use the trowel to smear, place and tap, then scrape the protruding mortar. The finishing touch was to wipe the bricks clean with a wet rag. When the mortar had a neat concave line between the bricks, it was time to recheck it with the plumb line.

The next Sunday there was a neat pile of timber. Dad brought his circular saw up from the work shed. This required a rather long extension cord that snaked from the lounge room window.

'You're not going to leave that blooming electric cord there for days on end, are you Max?'

'No, Else. I have no wish to die by electrocution.'

'A person doesn't need to be sarcastic, Max. Why did you have to take the screen off?'

'Didn't think you'd appreciate a hole in the flyscreen Else.'

'Humph. Certainly not!'

'Be more work for a person.'

The closing of the curtains demonstrated Mum's opinion on this further sarcasm.

Our neighbour, Guy Menzies, the builder who'd loaned Dad the cement mixer arrived and chatted amiably. 'Got an able apprentice there Max,' he said. 'Don't think any of my four boys will be following in my footsteps even though I've got 'Menzies and Sons' in huge letters on m'truck.'

'She's good alright. Never argues.'

'Don't know enough about it to argue, Dad,' I giggled.

Guy roared laughing. 'From what I've heard, you could argue about anything, Linda,' he chortled.

'Mr Menzies, what dreadful slander!' I protested with mock affront. 'I don't argue, I debate.'

'Ha! Ha!' he responded. 'Who do you think I am? If I don't know you, nobody does.'

I laughed.

'No,' he continued, 'my boys are all going to be bally scientists—or something. Always inventing things. The oldest is holed up in the shed doing 'electronics', whatever *that* is...'

Dad, who also had a strong interest in electronics was about to begin one of his rambling dissertations, but Mr Menzies was on a roll. 'Yeah, my shed smells of solder and David talks in another language—'diodes', 'capacitors' and God knows what else. If my John lives to see old bones I'll be a 'monkey's uncle'.'

Little did Dad know, the very soldering iron Mr Menzies was referring to was in fact Dad's, leased out to David by Peter, at an hourly rate. David had to come up with more money every time he wanted to work on his latest project. Our collective parents were not great believers in 'pocket money', referring to it as a 'rubbish American idea that would ruin children'. This meant any money we possessed had to be earned. The hard way—chores.

It was a wonderful day when the roller door went on the shed, officially turning it into that most coveted of neighbourhood possessions—The Garage.

'Hope you're not going to fill this with your stuff Max, and leave my car out in the rain,' said Mum.

'Mum!' I complained. 'Dad's done a perfect job!'

'He always does.'

'I helped.'

'So you did.'

Dad put some of his tools in the garage, neatly organised on Masonite board like the work shed, but the garage was always a garage, it never became another 'shed', in spite of Mum's fears. Whichever car we owned was never outside in all weathers.

One day Mum and I were going grocery shopping, a pleasure Dad was always happy to forgo. We were waiting for him to arrive and take the car out. He had appointed himself as the only one to drive in and out of the garage, muttering about its narrowness. This irked Mum no end. This particular day it was harder to bear, because she was in more of a hurry than usual. She rattled the keys in her hand and tapped the ground with an impatient foot.

Dad arrived and was still wiping grease off his hands.

'I don't know why you don't let me drive the jolly thing out. We've been waiting for eons,' Mum grated, looking at the keys as if considering the consequences of 'breaking Dad's rule'. A look of futility crossed her face. Perhaps she was remembering that whenever she'd undertaken something Dad had warned her about, things went to hell in a hand-basket. 'So you've got time in your busy schedule to drive the car out of the garage, but no time to come and help with the shopping.'

Hand on hip Mum jiggled the keys, reluctant to pass them over.

'Are you listening to me, Max?'

'Of course, Else.'

'What did I say, then?'

Dad fell into an uncomfortable silence.

'See!' said Mum, triumphantly.

'Now don't get a flea in your ear, Else.'

I flinched; there were few accusations that raised Mum's ire more than this. She jabbed the key brutally into the lock.

'Softly, softly, Else. Don't go at things like a bull at a gate!'

Naturally, this offended her even more. She thrust the garage door upwards with considerable strength—with the key still in the lock. There was a clunk as the key broke. The keyring and keys fell to the ground with a thud.

'See what happens when a person is pushed beyond endurance,' Mum muttered unrepentantly.

Dad looked silently to the heavens. Being his 'apprentice' I imagined him weighing his options. Would he need to drill the key out, or buy a new lock?

"Underbelly" comes to the suburbs

Not again! I couldn't believe it! Honestly what had I done in a former life??

Let me start at the beginning. I sometimes rent a room out, or two or three. It's part of my poverty management plan. I had to let my financial manager go, (oh alright, I never had one). Because I had my mother with me a couple of times to convalesce I hadn't had someone renting for a while so I accepted two guys who were working nearby and commuting interstate. I don't have a big house, but I've turned the lounge room into a bedsit.

Matthew, tenant/boarder No. 2 was a tall well built guy in his mid twenties with some really impressive looking tattoos, but a thoroughly gentle nature. He was easy going and relaxed, until... He arrived back from work one afternoon and sought me out while I was watering the garden.

'Do you know the phone number for the local police?' he asked, his eyes slits of steel.

I rattled it off quickly. His eyebrows rose at my instant reply. I shrugged. He hurried off to phone the cops. After he'd done that he came to chat, which loosely translated, meant turn the air blue about 'people' who had nothing better to do than thieve from hardworking men. And they were hard working; putting in twelve hour days, for eleven days straight, before having three days off. The thieves had picked the wrong guy on the wrong day. Suffice it to say that in recent times, 'life had been a bitch'. Well there was something about a bitch in there...

They had taken his GPS and about $500 worth of electronic gear he'd just bought. He had a mutter to his mates, then had a mutter to me. I told him about my episodes with 'Vandals and thieves' (see related stories) and I confided the name and location of the 'usual suspect'. I told him of the ongoing problems, electricity turned off, TV connections unplugged, bolts taken out, security lights broken, things stolen – the list seemed endless.

'Mmm,' said Matthew, 'might do a random walk around the neighbourhood, visit a few people. I'll see if anyone saw anything—and visit that kid.'

Now one doesn't offer advice to grown men renting rooms, but in the interest of the success of his mission I casually suggested he might have less trouble 'making his point' if his tattoos were clearly visible. To my surprise he went and changed into a muscle shirt. Off he went, his lithe 6 foot frame ramrod straight and determined. He was wearing his thin sunglasses. Only a single-celled amoeba would have missed his attitude. He had a casual chat with the neighbours on both sides, and across the road, and then he was out of sight. I went inside—he didn't need me staring after him, like a nervous puppy. He was back soon.

'Yeah, that kid's the one alright. Looked as guilty as sin as soon he opened the door.' Matthew went on to relate the rest of the conversation that had me gaping. Being around teenage boys and young men, I thought I'd heard everything. Apparently not.

'I told the little shit I'd be back in 30 minutes for my stuff and if it wasn't there I would &#*% him. I told him, 'I know people who know people' and if he wanted a peaceful life he'd leave this house alone for the rest of his miserable life.'

Oh crap, I thought. I'd been calm up to this point, but then my mind ran off to the reprisals I might suffer when these guys left. There were two men staying with a third guy arriving the next day on the same contract job. What then for me? What if I got it wrong? I would have chewed my nails, but I had none left. I said nothing, deciding to keep to myself for the designated 30 minutes. I nervously went back to watering. I was just washing up when Matthew came back through the door.

He was loaded up with all of his stolen stuff. I'm not often speechless, general anaesthetic being the only proven time, but that day my jaw was on the floor. Everything was in its original boxes and plastic bags.

'I suppose you're going to tell me you even got the receipts,' I said, when I found my voice.

'Better than that,' he said, lifting the lid of the cardboard box back to reveal some writing.

'I got the little creep to get a pen and write down the name of his friend and accomplice.'

My eyes were like saucers and his friend, the other boarder Deakin, came to the scene equally stunned. There on the box lid, was not only a name, but an address and phone number.

'I don't think the cops get this kind of result,' I mumbled.

'Still got to 'visit' the other prick,' said Matthew.

'Oh,' was all I could manage.

I wasn't privy to the details of the other visit—and quite frankly just wanted to lie down. A man's world belonged to a man, not a wuss like me.

Matthew and Deakin's friend, Danno arrived the next day. He had a huge double cabin Ute with logos and bull bars and other stuff—forgive me for the lack of information—I'm a girl. This guy was older and tougher, and sported even more impressive 'tatts'. The guys had a barbeque at the back, sat me down with a beer and recounted the story. With my head already swimming, I was glad for the beer. Matthew and Danno went for a drive. Danno's arrival couldn't have been timed better. After Matthew's subtle statement that 'he knew people who knew people' it must have looked like the 'big boss from out of town' had arrived.

Matthew and Danno arrived back to say they'd visited the culprits again because the security codes for Matthew's gear was missing.

'I think we scared the crap out of the whole family,' said Matthew.

'Certainly made the father shit himself,' said Danno.

I didn't know how much more excitement I could take. The thought that, for once, someone bigger was on my side was strangely exhilarating. Terrifying, but definitely exhilarating. I tried to turn off the side of my brain worrying how it could all go terribly wrong, and enjoy the moment.

'I'm living in 'Underbelly', only on the right side,' I exclaimed. They all grinned.

The next day I opened the door to a strange man. He appeared to be trembling slightly. He introduced himself as the father of one of the boys. He wanted to know if I could ask Matthew to phone him and handed me his mobile number. Slightly emboldened by having 'back up' for the first time in history I announced that it 'wasn't my business', but I didn't think Matthew would want to waste valuable mobile phone time on someone who'd already ripped him off.

'Why don't you come back when they're home?' I suggested helpfully.

He appeared to put this idea on a par with being alone with a hungry crocodile and began jabbering on with other options.

'You really have to speak to Matthew,' I said. 'I'm just the landlady.' I looked a little blank.

'Of course, these boys have been vandalising and stealing from me in the past, so personally I am going to apply for AVOs so they stay away from my property. But that's just me.'

'Get up here!' he yelled over his shoulder.

I looked down to the car and there were the two culprits. How had I missed that? They came quickly to the door. They all apologised, gave me their mobile phone numbers and gratefully left.

If the boarders were chuffed when I referred to them as 'The Underbelly Crew', they didn't show it. I wondered how it would be when they left. To my astonishment not a single leaf on a tree was touched.

Fireball

When I first met Adam, in the late 1980s, he constantly regaled me with the hilarious stories of his own childhood mishaps. Of how he had been tangled in the barbed wire fence that kept the goats in and had to be removed by the fire brigade.

It was hard to imagine this youthful clumsiness in a handsome man with the physique and energy of an athlete. He gave the appearance of physical control. I was soon to discover he hadn't outgrown his ability for disaster.

One day not long before we were married, Adam took eleven year old Luke to the local creek for a swim. They found a rope swing and proceeded to do what boys do.

When they arrived home, Adam was covered in bruises and scratches from head to toe, but Luke didn't have a mark on him. Luke, who is a master at saying nothing, said nothing, and said it very well. It was years before he would be moved to comment, 'he's an idiot', but back then he said nothing.

We were treated to an extremely lengthy account by Adam of how it was the tree's fault, an epistle that I am sorry to say, we all found very amusing.

For a long time after we indulged in lengthy discussions, accompanied by much hilarity and snorting, on how the tree had shifted, and various hurricane-inspired conspiracy theories were developed, much to the Adam's disgust and disdain. He would respond, 'You people don't know what you are talking about.' We never did.

However Adam's 'piece de resistance' was when he blew up my laundry. This took place several months after we were married. Adam had a favourite shirt and he had worn it when helping 'fix' his brother-in-law's car. I don't think the car ever went again.

The shirt had so much grease it was hard to tell its previous colour. Even so, Adam was not very impressed when he found it in the rubbish bin—relegated there by me. After more-than-a-little preaching about my laundry skills, and general lack of respect for a man's property, he proceeded to use kerosene to get the stains out.

Kerosene, he proclaimed, had unrivalled effectiveness to remove grease. He then found he couldn't get the kerosene and its odour out. By this time, a whole load of washing had also been contaminated by the kerosene from the soaked shirt.

After a bit more lecturing Adam moved on to remove the kerosene from the whole wash by using petrol as a, God help me, 'solvent'. He carried the jerry can full of petrol into the laundry and rinsed the whole sink full of clothes with it before pouring copious amounts of sudsy water over them in an attempt to, yes, get the petrol out.

I walked into the room as he was putting the whole sorry mess in the washing machine. On this occasion I took a leaf out of Luke's book and said nothing. After all, I'd heard enough lectures for one day. Ironically, one had centred on Adam's expertise and experience as a Volunteer Fire Fighter in Victoria.

The washing machine began to fill, and for once in my life I decided that discretion was the better part of valour and walked out of the room. The washing machine started. The electricity sparked. The laundry went off like a bomb. A fire ball followed me out the door.

He was dead; I knew it. I did what all practical women do in such a crisis. I screamed. I was immobilized by fear. Not Adam, however. After what seemed like hours, but was probably only a few seconds he streaked out of the laundry yelling instructions like a warlord. Still numb with shock, I didn't understand a word he was yelling.

He ran outside. He ran inside. He ran outside again. He ran back into the laundry where there was a nice combination of fire, electricity and water. He grabbed the jerry can that by this time had flames coming out of the top and ran outside again. Obviously not content with his earlier near brush with death he was determined to put paid to his existence further endangering his life by carrying a potential bomb supplied by the huge lethal flaming jerry can.

Meanwhile the fracas attracted the children, eleven year old Luke and Adam's daughter, Sarah who was 15. Luke frowned and went outside to the meter box and turned the electricity off. In retrospect this was the only sensible action of the day. Suddenly the realisation that Adam was not dead and was in fact quite vocal sank in and propelled me into action.

I ordered him into a cold bath and then organised the kids to go to the neighbours, who were by now ringing the local mines to ask why they were dynamiting so close to houses, to get ice or anything frozen. So there he sat, naked from the waist down, in the bath with broccoli, peas and raspberries, still able to sound forth on how we were all useless, prone to panic and had no idea what to do in a crisis.

His legs looked suspiciously red so I phoned the ambulance. The ambulance arrived and an officer with rounded girth, and bunched muscles, crossed his arms and surveyed a half-naked Adam in the frozen soup bath. The fire department and police weren't needed because Luke had thrown my favourite blanket over the fire.

'Well sunshine, what have we here?' asked the ambulance officer, with a decided smirk wreathing his face.

Adam informed him that he was fine '*thank you very much* and couldn't comprehend what had possessed his *overreacting* wife to phone them.'

'Stand up and show me sunshine.'

Sunshine stood up.

He was not so fine without the ice water. His red angry legs wobbled as the blow torch effect of the burns set in. His face paled as he sunk back into the soupy bath.

'I think we better take you to the doctor, sunshine.'

Sunshine went.

On the way out the door I suggested that he might want to accept pain relief. Adam pompously informed me that he would need no such thing. He was not a drug addict like me, who took pain relief for migraines or any old disc pain.

I was told later that by the time Adam got to the surgery he had howled like a baby and begged for pethidine. The ambulance officer wouldn't give it to him because of his pompous rant to me.

The doctor took pity on Adam and gave him an injection for pain. He was admitted to the local private hospital for observation and treatment of his burns and stayed over a week. After daily dressings and assessment when the blisters subsided it was determined that his burns were 'second degree' and not full thickness.

He had narcotic injections several times and *no-one* called *him* a drug addict. He took the opportunity in his new calm horizontal state to read a heavy tome by Paul Tournier, the French psychiatrist and theologian, claiming to benefit greatly from his enforced stay, with the faint suggestion it had 'elevated his thinking'.

I liked him very much in his new mellow state. Initially I didn't want to worry him by discussing all the cleaning up and expense, but his new found peace and euphoria soon began to annoy me, so I told him about *all* of the work and expenses we were facing.

'It's only money,' he said floatingly, from his lofty vantage point.

This waffle from the same man, who once lectured me for more than an hour, on the economic advantages and expense involved in purchasing the 500g Weet-Bix packet, which was the only size he would endorse.

The Great Escape

We holidayed in caravans. And by caravans, I mean tiny round rejects that Dad gutted and rebuilt. While conveying these ramshackle carcasses behind our pristine sedan, Dad thoroughly enjoyed the dubious stares of others.

Even Mum, who usually knew better than to doubt Dad's prowess said, 'What the heck is that, Max?' when Dad brought the first one home.

'Are you casting aspersions on your future holiday residence, Elsie?'

Mum wiped her hands on her apron and went inside.

'Good grief, Dad. It looks like a whale skeleton,' I said.

'You've got an imagination there Bub, I'll give you that.'

Work on the derelict frame began in earnest. Plywood sheets arrived. Extension cords criss-crossed the yard. My sixteen year old brother Peter was eager to help. Dad planed the curved surfaces after they were placed.

'How's the surface going, son?'

Peter ran a practised hand over the timber. 'Feels pretty smooth, Dad.'

'Good.'

There was a load of washing to put on the line, but as usual Dad's projects held greater appeal for me than any form of domesticity. 'Can I...?'

'You'd be a help if you tied Snoopy somewhere else, sis,' said Peter.

'Aw, leave off! He's too strong for me. He runs round in circles, winds the chain around my legs and pulls me over.' I eyed Snoopy with reluctance, and received his usual tongue-lolling grin. 'Anyway, where'll I put him? There's only the clothesline and I have to hang the washing out.'

Peter rolled his eyes. Dad looked up, and pointed to the back step where Mum stood, hands on hips.

'Washing won't hang itself, Linda,' she said. 'You'd forget your head if it wasn't screwed on. Leave the men alone.'

Mum smiled at "the men" with pride. Not for her the nagging of weary wifedom over half-completed projects strewn across backyards for years. Dad finished what he started. If Mum ever complained he was taking too long we kids started an uproar, 'Fair go, Mum. You've gotta be kidding!'

I don't know how Dad managed it, but these rejects from the junk yard became palaces. Everything in them was tailored for space and function. Cupboards were added overhead, in corners and under beds. With the speed of a conjurer Dad transformed the layout at night, making beds appear where the dining table had held pride of place.

'What a marvel,' Mum said, when it was finally complete with fridge and gas cooker.

Then it was her turn. Curtains and trimmings were added. If any of us thought Dad had overdone things, Mum took caravanning to a whole new level. With skill that defied reason 'holiday' food was no different than home. Baked treats were daily fare. Domesticity still prevailed in my mother's world. She recreated "home".

The ignorance of childhood made this seem like magic. I think it was one way Mum could take the familiarity of her life with her. However, there was time for recreation. Mum and I did jigsaw puzzles together. Crouched solemnly over the laminate table we each worked on one side of the map of Australia that was her favourite. There was none of the hilarity and thigh slapping that accompanied the games of strategy like draughts and Chinese checkers Dad and I played. We once made a single game of draughts last for two hours, much to Mum's disgust.

We holidayed around Lake Macquarie, often spending weekends at Shingle Splitters, a point that juts into the saltwater lake dividing it into a calm haven on one side and a windswept reedy curve on the other. Sometimes the wind turned, its mercurial gusts rampaging both sides. Cobalt-green water crimped in midday breezes as it lapped with metronomic lyric on creamy sand. Tall pines extended to the end of the point. A hilly area where eucalypts, pines and scrub gathered indifferently allowed children a secret domain, where shrieks of 'You're it, tagged ya' echoed over the water.

Then it all changed. The speedboats came with their growling engines, gleaming fibreglass perfection, water thumping speeds, mile-wide wakes and spitting spray. They heralded a new kind of weekender—water skiers. Our peace was ruined, our favourite place had gone to the dogs. Even Mum ceased her crossword in the shade of a tree to squint at the newcomers and mutter, 'Hmmph'.

Dad got an inscrutable glint in his eye. He and Peter took off on trips to the marina at Toronto.

'Crikey, Max,' said Mum, 'you're not looking at those fancy expensive boats are you? In our dreams!'

But, come summer, we were the proud owners of a sleek speed boat with a gutsy roar, and dashing blue strip Dad had meticulously painted. It spewed smoke with the best of them. So we learned to ski—and by that I mean my brother Peter morphed into James Bond, while I survived as long as the boat went in straight lines, which didn't happen much. Off I went—careening at a perfect tangent to the trajectory of the boat, where I sank in ignominy and had to be pulled aboard spluttering, with my life jacket choking me.

After a day on the water we happily returned to our caravan, where there was balm for our stinging skin, rest for our aching muscles, and food, glorious food. Free from the endless chores of home, I never wanted the holidays to end.

'Mum,' I said one evening, 'we have everything we need, don't we?'

'Of course.'

'Well, we haven't really missed anything from home … so…'

'What are you getting at, Linda?'

'Maybe we could throw a whole heap of stuff out when we get home and there'd be less to do?' I gave her my most ingratiating smile. It was a hard sell.

'Honestly Linda,' she said, 'sometimes I don't know where you came from.'

Northern Territory

Never mind Jimmy Cook
Never mind all that fable
the Indonesians were first
to sit at our table

The Great Southern Land
neither conquered nor fought
but free trade arrangements
for trepang were sought

Never mind Alfie Deakin
Never Mind Georgie the Five
there in the vast north land
was an industry hive

Without cabinet ministers
writs or ICAC flaws
tens of thousands lived
within our fair shores

Never mind the Kimberly plan
Never mind the **un**promised land
exquisite beauty hidden
in timeless red-dust sand

Kakadu, Uluru, Kata Tjuta
what vision, what glory
in long-snaked river, in Arafura
and Arnhem land story

Australia

Stretched summer days
chill of cool water
kissing sting of sun
floating, drifting
endless white sand
trees shade saltwater lakes
midnight phosphorescence

timeless spaces
wind-carved deep ravines
red-orange, blue-purple
tulle fuschia-skirted bottlebrush
orange-furred kangaroo paw
wax flower, cowslip orchid
flame grevillea, hooded lily

rain on tin rooftops
zig zag mountain trails
buildings curve into landscape
high rise cityscapes
sharpen horizons
interrupted by ocean

endless washed-pale cerulean skies
joyful splash of wattle
eucalypts crowd shorelines
towns crouch on coastlines

red-brick sliced mountain ranges
flaunting dark green treed cliffs,
surrounded by sea, green cobalt
amber-bright dawns
Nullarbor dreaming greets treeless horizon
red dust meets turquoise dessert sky
grey-green low succulents

salt-washed beach grasses
children sliding on cardboard sleds
down terraced sand hills
Australia

Billabong

willows trail
tear-stranded chains
in the mud-brown water
at the creek's elbow
where we once played
on bleached summer days
giggling and hiding
deep within its playful strands
caring naught
when moss-slimed roots jutted
from yielding clay-bedded banks
into shadowy water beneath
their velvety strength
forged there, fixed, resolute.

How pale the tiny lime-bright leaves
shielding from summer storms' lash
that flashed then faded.

How forgiving the branches
as we clung and swayed.

How easily they were persuaded
to join our childish leaping
as we danced like water elves
singing summer's last song.

Peter Wilson

Peter Wilson is a thoughtful poet whose work reveals a unique knowledge of the human condition. Peter's poetry is measured and courageous, insightful and deep.

Nev – A True Mate

There isn't much of Nev but what there is it counts,
lean and hard as sprung steel with as much energy and bounce.

He's a man of the land with a nature straight and true,
so if you're in a spot of bother, then Nev's the mate for you.

He's been around a fair while and he knows the land by heart,
a legend in his own time but he's not ready to depart.

He's been there- and done that and is liked and loved by all
and our lives in comparison, just seem to fade and pall.

So where did he come from, this icon at our side?
Was he born on Aussie soil, or did he come for the ride?

Study Nev – look really hard and you can see his Scots descent
but he was born a farmer's son and did his share to pay the rent.

Born in the far north country with the red soil as his bed,
he's the backbone of the nation and a hero; all things said.

Old and gnarled he may be but the spring's still in his stride.
He'll be your mate forever 'til God calls him to his side.

The Settler's Tale

When I look upon my neighbours I'm amazed at what I see,
all colours, hues and races living here in harmony

We're all proud to be Australians we make this country great,
but where is the 'true blue Aussie', the one who calls you mate?

They're here alright, alive and well you see them every day,
on the streets, in supermarkets at work, at prayer or play

Not loud or ostentatious dignified - not grand
all the heritage of this nation proud of belonging to this land

All with iron will and courage coping as only they knew how,
fed and clothed their offspring who lacked for little, then and now

Their success is in their children the fruit of lean but happy years
a father's vision of manly pride in mother's eyes those joyous tears

When you're wondering who *our country's heroes are*, and where,
look at those next to you, these are true blue Aussies there.

Peter Wilson

The Black of Night

I gaze into the inky black as peace descends and freezes time.
As life's intricacies lose their track I feel at one with nature's rhyme.

The yawning darkness slowly sinks, enveloping my watchful sense.
My mind embraces this new world that steals my last defence.

The dark void opens up its arms Encompassing a peaceful shroud
and I succumb to its charms as it spreads its dark winged cloud.

Glittering points of silvery ice, jewels in the velvet sky
born trembling, in the black of night before dissolving before my eye.

Insidiously my heart rate slows as I absorb this tranquil sight,
until saturated with an inner glow I lose all sight of fear and flight.

I sink into an inner calm, my heart slows its pulsing beat.
The darkness is a soothing balm that cools emotion's troubled heat.

Slowly, as a bud unfolds a mystical display of light
magnificent, bright and bold emerges from the black of night.

And as I concentrate my gaze I see beyond the edge of sight.
Illuminated in the moon's silvery haze, a millionfold points of light.

With the advance of dawn's weak glow the magic of the night receded
I wonder, as I slowly waken was it but a dream that preceded?

www.ingramcontent.com/pod-product-compliance
Lightning Source LLC
Chambersburg PA
CBHW031414290426
44110CB00011B/370